Pearls
Parenting Practices

**Relayed Through Stories, Illustrations,
Affirmations, Poems, and Quotes**

Lisa Guy

Illustrated by Cameron Shields

Library of Congress Control Number: 2023913369

ISBN 979-8-9887106-1-5

Printed in the United States of America
First printing August 2023

Dedications

Lisa Guy

I dedicate this book to my father, Ronald Anthony Pellegrino. Throughout my life, he made me feel valued, capable, and important – even when I was very young. A creative, accomplished, and curious man, my father loved nothing more than children, music, art, and learning. May this book honor his memory and provide valuable guidance to many new parents and caregivers, as they prioritize their children and do what they can to help them grow into the very best possible version of themselves.

Cameron Shields

Dedicated to my father and mother, who taught me the value of perspective in both drawing and life.

Introduction

The ideas for this book were inspired by the past thirty years as my children have been growing up, moving out into the world, and beginning to look toward the future, which includes having children of their own. My husband Keith and I had our first of four daughters in December of 1989, and at the time Kathryn was born I had never held a baby. I was working full-time at our mortgage company in Southern California and had just finished a 12-hour day when I went into labor.

Leading up to Kathryn's birth, Keith and I had prepared as best we could, but it's hard to describe the gravity of emotion we both felt the day Kathryn was born. Keith had left the hospital for a short time to bring me some clothes, and as he was heading back to us, he had to pull the car over. The magnitude of bringing a child into the world was almost more than he could bear. We had so much to learn!

Eleven years and three additional daughters later, our son William was born, and I felt excited, empowered, confident and thoroughly prepared. I kept thinking, "If only I had known half of what I know now when Kathryn was born."

It is hard to find the time to read once a little one arrives, and new parents and caregivers may have had minimal experience with children. It is my hope that this book will convey encouragement, insight, and confidence, and in addition, provide practical information and principles for a positive parenting experience. It is a gift to both the new baby and parent/ caregiver, <u>to be read aloud daily over a period of time</u> while cuddling and sharing special moments together. In this way, the habit of reading, talking, connecting and relaxing with your child will become a regular practice – quickly and naturally. The gifts of reading, connection and learning cannot be understated, and will give children the best possible chance in life when carried out regularly.

Research shows that infants growing up in a verbally rich environment have a huge advantage right from the start, and one of the best things a parent can give to a child is time spent together in open and honest communication.[1] Affirmations and quotes on the left-side pages are meant to be read aloud to Baby, and parents may choose to read the supporting stories and quotes (collected from a variety of parents, caregivers, and professionals in my community on the Central Coast, and beyond) on the right-hand pages aloud or to themselves.

PEARLS evolves from the early parenting practices of infants, to what really matters in life as we grow older. The first five years of childhood have been found to be the most impactful for future development, but parents and caregivers with children of any age can glean knowledge and insight from the chapters of this book. Illustrator Cameron Shields has captured the magical quality of the Central Coast, and the feelings of love embedded in each illustration provide readers with a sense of peace and calm. May meaningful seeds be planted in the minds of parents/caregivers and young children as the ideas of this book are relayed and the affirmations are spoken aloud.

 Look for the pearls in each section!

*Please remember the ideas, suggestions, and concepts contained in this book are not meant to replace the advice of your health care provider.

Just as a pearl is formed over time, beginning with a tiny grain of sand, a child evolves gradually, and is shaped by the countless experiences he or she has from birth to adulthood. Understanding the importance of this gradual process, loving our children unconditionally, and making the most of each day with them, can prove invaluable to their successful development.

As new parents and caregivers read the affirmations and quotes aloud to baby on the pages that follow, the words themselves will have meaning for parents only, but their rhythm and cadence will be taken in eagerly – as a gift of language and love for all new little ones.

Contents

Introduction   *i*

Chapter 1:

Parenting of Infants – Challenges   1
    & Guidance During the Early Months

Chapter 2:

Early Practices – Ways to Ensure Well-Being of   16
    Both Baby and Parents

Chapter 3:

Authoritative (not Authoritarian) Parenting – Ongoing   32
    Communication and Good Habits Work Together to Foster
    Healthy, Well-balanced Children

Chapter 4:

Raising Connected Children – Purpose & Meaning   52
    Come from a Sense of Unity

Chapter 5:

Life Perspective –The Way We Parent and View the World   72
    Will Have a Lasting Impact on Our Developing Child

Chapter 6:

Satisfaction and Fulfillment –   94
    What Truly Matters

Chapter 1

Parenting of Infants – Challenges
and Guidance During the Early Months

Life at Home Begins

Growing up as a young girl in the Midwest, I had a childhood filled with freedom, adventure, imagination, and lots of outdoor physical activity. The only downside was our frequent moves every several years, which at the time caused me a great deal of stress. Looking back, I realize that the stability and love my parents gave me from an early age made it possible for me to overcome my fears each time we moved. This allowed me to have the confidence and resilience to walk into new situations, meet new people, master new systems and ultimately thrive.

My parents were young when they had me. It took them some time to become comfortable with a new baby. Soon our nuclear family of three fell into a smooth routine, with daily walks and outside playtime, family meals, and music, songs and stories at bedtime. Twenty-six years later, my husband and I arrived home with our new little bundle, and the realization that she depended solely and completely on us was daunting, but we were determined to do our best to recognize and satisfy her needs.

The biggest struggles early on were mastering the art of breast feeding – which no one had told me could be so painful at first – and establishing a rhythm to our days and nights. I remember experiencing a vast number of emotions as my hormones fluctuated wildly, and my world was turned upside down.

Each section of this book represents a concept, idea or practice which has had a significant impact on my journey as a parent. My hope is that many other new mothers and fathers will benefit from the wisdom, support and guidance these ideas offer.

Prioritize your new baby, and make a commitment to continually learn, explore, communicate and enjoy. . . and remember, the childhood years are finite!

Hold your baby, nurture and play with your baby, read and speak to your baby, and above all else, love your baby.

~ Lisa Guy

Welcome Home Section 1

Welcome home, my precious one,
  A thousand hopes, and dreams, and fears…

We dreamt of you, my little one
And now you're here...

Isn't it wonderful?

"'Home' is the nicest word there is." ~ Laura Ingalls Wilder, Writer

Welcome Home

"You can never spoil a baby." ~ Dr. Lou Tedone, Father of 9, Pediatrician

The most critical role that new parents play is protecting and caring for their tiny human being.

It has always amazed me that there are no courses, tests, degrees or certifications required to bring a baby into this world. The number of parenting books written is staggering, but in reality, what new parent has much time to read? Parenting is an art, and "learn by doing" is the process of mastering this most important endeavor. The most critical role a new parent plays is protecting and caring for their tiny human being. Identifying and satisfying needs is of the utmost importance, and when babies cry, it is up to the parents or caregivers to figure out what it is they require.

Remember, it is not possible to spoil a baby by holding him or her too much. It's essential to build trust with your newborn, conveying a feeling of physical and emotional safety. Additionally, parents should understand that touch is vital to a baby's growth and development! ~ Lisa Guy; Age 58; 5 Children; Former Business Owner/Writer/Community Volunteer

Take care to protect your new, vulnerable little one!

My advice to new parents while children are still infants, is to "baby proof" the home, remembering to do the same for the homes of babysitters and grandparents. In doing so, it is imperative to lock up medications, cleaning products, sharp objects, firearms, and anything else which could be dangerous for a young, inquisitive child. Remember to watch for items belonging to older children, including toys or books which contain small batteries. Be sure to avoid anything that may contain lead – during my many years as a pediatrician, I have treated a number of children who have suffered unnecessarily from lead poisoning.

A great resource for parents is HealthyChildren.org[1] – it contains all current information from the American Academy of Pediatrics. Additionally, parents would be wise to access and review a product recall website[2] – especially if any baby items are second hand. Many parents don't know that babies should never be exposed to direct sunlight – please take care to protect your new, vulnerable little one! ~ Kathleen Long, M.D.; 2 Children; 3 Grandchildren; Pediatrician

Rhythm and Babies Section 2

Don't you worry,
we will find
a rhythm to settle into…
with pleasant days and peaceful nights.

Won't that be nice?

Toddlers thrive on regular rhythm. They like the predictability of knowing what is happening now and what is coming next. It provides them with a feeling of safety and security.
~ Simone Davies,
The Montessori Toddler[3]

Rhythm and Babies

Parents can follow the cues of their newborn to establish a rhythm and schedule that works for the entire family.

I created a daily rhythm and routine for my children by following my newborn's cues. We fed, slept, played, and cuddled according to my newborn's schedule. As each of my children grew and began to establish their own circadian rhythms, our family routine worked around my infant's, as well as our older childrens' routines that had gradually evolved over the years. Our family organically adjusted to each other's needs and patterns and soon we had a regular family routine. I tried to do things similarly each day, but sometimes we mixed it up out of necessity or fun. On these occasions it might take us some time to get back into the swing of things, but my family learned resiliency and flexibility as well as loving our normal daily patterns. I found that instead of forcing my kids into my preconceived schedule, I modified my life around their rhythms, and things went much more smoothly for everyone.

When new parents ask me, "When can I get my child onto a schedule?" I genuinely say, "You will learn to follow your baby's schedule. Your baby will create a routine all on their own, and that is the easiest way to establish a routine to your day." Why fight upstream? If we respond to our infant's hunger, sleep and play cues, we will co-create a natural rhythm to our days. ~Lisa Boyd, IBCLC, LCCE; 3 Children; Postpartum Doula & Lactation Consultant

Developing a consistent routine early on provides infants with a sense of safety and security.

It takes infants approximately two to four months to establish a circadian rhythm. Developing healthy "light habits" including exposure to daylight (for optimum production of melatonin) and eliminating artificial blue light from cell phones, TV, and computers at night, can help infants (and parents) to settle into a comfortable daily rhythm. It is helpful to establish a regular feeding and bath schedule, with activity during the daylight hours and peaceful routines at night. Reading, rocking, and singing help to calm both child and parent. ~ Lisa Guy

Newborns can benefit from the rhythm of gentle movement.

Movement and rhythm were magically effective in comforting my newborns. For each of my five babies, being placed over my shoulder, with gentle pats on the back, would generally result in instant calm and all would be well. Our youngest daughter suffered from colic early on, and I spent many nights with her in the stroller, pushing her gently over the cobblestones in our neighborhood. The rhythmic vibration was soothing and led her to fall into a deep sleep. Many of my friends were able to comfortably "wear" their babies in front- or back-packs for a number of months, mimicking their time in utero. ~ Lisa Guy

Advice Section 3

Y ou are loved
and your arrival brings such joy!

We may receive advice
from those who mean well,
and if we do,
we'll listen with an open mind
and trust our intuition to guide us
confidently and without guilt.

Isn't this good to know?

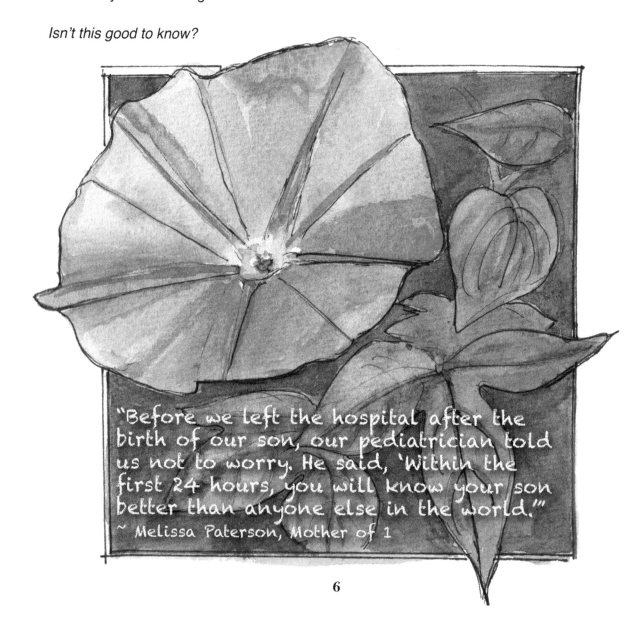

"Before we left the hospital after the birth of our son, our pediatrician told us not to worry. He said, 'Within the first 24 hours, you will know your son better than anyone else in the world.'"
~ Melissa Paterson, Mother of 1

Advice

 ***Parents and caregivers can feel comfortable following their own intuition.***

My 11-month-old daughter was unable to latch properly when breastfeeding early on and I felt sure there was a problem. After a referral to one of the top-ranked lactation consultants in the area, we found that my baby did, in fact, have a condition referred to as "lip and tongue tie" – a restriction of the upper lip/tongue which tethers it to the roof/floor of the mouth, resulting in limited mobility and difficulty in nursing. After diagnosing the problem, our lactation consultant then connected us with one of the best dentists in the area who specializes in lip and tongue tie revisions. Immediately following the revision, Elle was able to latch without pain.

I knew that nursing was important to the long-term health of my baby, and I was prepared to do whatever I could to breastfeed her. As a new mother, I received a plethora of information, advice, and conflicting opinions. I have come to realize how important it is to follow my own intuition and seek out opinions from a variety of professionals when the need arises. I feel incredibly blessed that I had the A+ team of formidable women helping me through my challenging postpartum journey with kindness, respect, and empathy. ~ Caitlin Hager; Age 32; 1 Child; former College Volleyball Coach

Parents and caregivers can research areas of concern, seek and listen to advice, and ultimately make their own parenting choices.

I was completely unprepared for the excruciating pain of breastfeeding and the exhaustion and discomfort of a newborn who was looking to suck around the clock! My son had difficulty latching properly early on, and as a result my nipples were cracked and bleeding. Intuitively I felt that offering my son a pacifier was the answer, but I had been advised by several people early on who were adamant a pacifier should NEVER be given before four weeks. After just a few days home from the hospital with my son, I became desperate – I was in so much pain, nursing constantly and feeling guilty. It wasn't until a family friend with 5 children came to visit, that I had the courage to follow my gut. Both she and my mom encouraged me to offer him a pacifier – finally I felt I'd been given permission to listen to my own intuition and the needs of my body and baby. I have since come to find that while it is important to maintain an inquisitive mind, research areas of concern prior to making important decisions, and listen to the advice of seasoned parents and professionals, ultimately the parenting choices are mine and my husband's to make. ~ Aubrey Semenova; Age 32; 3 Children; Registered Nurse

Note: The La Leche League[4] has some suggestions on ways to avoid nipple confusion.

Feeding Baby Section 4

We will treasure the time we spend together each day
while you receive the nourishment you need
to grow healthy and strong.

We know it won't be long
before you're eating on your own
and flitting everywhere you go.
But for now,
we'll cherish
this special time together.

Let's relax and enjoy!

"It's important to understand that most substances and medications make their way into mother's milk. The legalization of marijuana has created confusion, and the long-term effect on developing children has emerged as being detrimental to normal neurodevelopment. It is best to avoid marijuana (as well as alcohol and other drugs not prescribed by a doctor) while breastfeeding."
~ Dawn Wilt, Registered Dietitian, International Board-Certified Lactation Consultant

Feeding Baby

Ideally, babies should be given only breast milk or formula during the first six months.

Because our gut microbiome is established early on, proper nutrition during childhood is essential and plays a lasting role in the long-term health of our bodies. Studies have shown that breast milk has many benefits, including lowering the risk of allergies, and asthma. I come from a generation whose mothers were told that formula was the "modern way" to feed babies. I believe our current society should do all we can to encourage mothers to breastfeed, while balancing the message of its benefits with empathy, and supporting moms who try their best but are unable to feed their babies this precious food. Parents must be aware of the significant health benefits of breast milk, while understanding that breastfeeding is just a tiny part of parenting. Through the years, there are thousands of opportunities to give to, and guide, our children. ~ Wendy Fertschneider; Age 64; 1 Child; Registered Dietitian, Public Health Nutritionist

★   ★   ★

Seeking help from a lactation specialist can be helpful.

As a pediatric nurse practitioner who has worked with families for over 40 years, I have seen just about every breastfeeding challenge. Breastfed babies behave differently than bottle-fed babies in their first 3 months of life – they signal more to their parents about their hunger, take longer to eat, and are fed more often. Parents who don't understand normal newborn behaviors and the dynamics of breastfeeding may believe their infants are not getting the nourishment they need to thrive and may choose to begin feeding formula. I help new mothers to recognize and respond to early baby-need cues, and how to effectively meet the needs of their babies. ~ Andrea Herron; 1 Child; Author, RN, MN, CPNP, IBCLC

★   ★   ★

There are many ways to parent a child – what matters most are connection and love.

After over 15 years of working with new parents and raising my own three children, I have come to realize that what matters most is following your heart, however you decide to parent your child. For some that may be going back to work, day care, formula feeding and sleep training (as my sister chose), and for others it may mean extended breastfeeding, staying home, homeschooling, and following our children's circadian rhythms (as I have chosen). We both have wonderful kids and amazing relationships with them, but we went about parenting completely differently, because WE are so different! If we all can parent in a way that feels authentic to us, and focus on loving, respecting, and honoring our children while having open communication and supporting them on their own paths, our children will thrive. We will have fewer disconnected children, fewer drug and mental health disorders, and a stronger society. Connection and love are what our children need most. ~ Lisa Boyd; IBCLC, LCCE; 3 Children; Postpartum Doula & Lactation Consultant

Promoting Calm and Sleep Section 5

Sleep, my precious, sleep,
for this is the time
when your brain and body
will grow the most.

Sleep is important to us as well,
and we will try to rest when you do,
letting housework and other chores
go for now -
knowing that being with you
is most important.

Shall we close our eyes?

"Sleep is that golden
chain that ties
health and our
bodies together."
~ Thomas Dekker, English Poet

Promoting Calm and Sleep

Always put Baby to bed in a calm state, not yet quite asleep, and on his or her back!

During my many years as a pediatrician, sleep has been the number one issue raised by parents at their child's 1 year check-up. By this time, many bad habits have been established. From my experience it's simple: From the very beginning, establish a schedule for your infant and always put Baby to bed in a calm state, not yet quite asleep, and on his or her back! When babies become accustomed to falling asleep on their own, in their own safe and special bed, they are able to self-soothe if they awaken and trust that a loved one will come to find them if necessary. ~ Kathleen Long, MD; 2 Children; 3 Grandchildren; Pediatrician

Parents can use the 5 S's to calm Baby and prepare for sleep.

Our oldest daughter had problems sleeping early on, and my husband and I were struggling. I had heard of a pediatric sleep specialist from out of town, and I enlisted her help. The guidance she gave us was invaluable. She also encouraged me to become certified myself, so I could help others on the Central Coast. Dealing with the trials of life is so much easier on a full night of sleep! I explain to parents that the first 3 months after birth are considered the fourth trimester, and the "5 S's," as they are called, can be tremendously helpful in soothing a newborn baby, especially during this time. The 5 S's are: shushing, side lying (in parent or caregivers' arms), swaddling, sucking, and swinging - all things which serve to turn on a baby's soothing mechanism. Some babies might need one or two of these, while others may need all five at the same time to calm down. ~ Kerrin Edmonds; Age 37; 3 Children; Pediatric Sleep Specialist

Parents and caregivers can choose the sleep method which works best for their families.

Sleep is a hot topic for many new parents! Some embrace "attachment parenting," which suggests that babies do not need to be trained or taught how to sleep. Parents allow Baby to fall asleep at breast or contact nap so they can respond to and be in close contact with their little one both day and night. Others embrace "sleep training," which incorporates a less breastfeeding-friendly "feed, play, sleep" model with long spans of sleep. This approach works better with bottle feeding. I am very sensitive to the topic of sleep, as I struggled with society's expectations versus my own innate need to be close to my child and parent the way that felt right to us both. In the end, I went against the grain, following my children's circadian rhythms, and embracing natural term breastfeeding with child-led weaning. My kids didn't sleep through the night until they were older, but it worked for us. Some good advice I received years ago was to "start with the end in mind." I encourage new parents to think carefully about their family goals and let their hearts be their guide. ~ Lisa Boyd; IBCLC, LCCE; 3 Children; Postpartum Doula & Lactation Consultant

Establishing Routines & Dividing Responsibilities Section 6

We have many new routines and adjustments to make.
Soon all will begin to come naturally.

When possible, our family will divide responsibilities
and share in work and play,
bringing us together -
keeping us aligned and joyful.

When necessary,
we will look outside our immediate family
for help, guidance, and support.

Aren't we lucky to have loved ones in our lives who care?

> "No parent can single-handedly meet a child's need for love."
> ~ Gary Chapman and Ross Campbell
> in The 5 Love Languages of Children:
> The Secret to Loving Children
> Effectively[5]

Establishing Routines and Dividing Responsibilities

We can divide parenting duties to the best benefit of both the parents and child.

As parents and caregivers, we can work together to split up duties, keeping in mind our own aptitudes and preferences, yet understanding there will likely be responsibilities outside our areas of comfort. Working on tasks we find challenging can be helpful to both our children and us – especially during the early months when there are many ways for all involved to contribute! Three weeks after we brought our newborn daughter home, I learned that my husband, who is a wonderful daytime dad, is a less-than-effective nighttime father. I woke up with a start on his "nightshift" to find my husband beside himself as our infant howled. Understanding he was unable to care for her appropriately at that moment, I took her in my arms and gently calmed her.

Six months later, when it was time to train our daughter to sleep through the night, I asked my mother-in-law if she could have a visit with my husband and son at her home until the training was complete. I knew that neither could stand to hear our baby cry, and while they were home, any progress toward her self-soothing would be impossible. Within a week, she was sleeping through the night and my husband and son were able to rejoin us. Over the years my husband and I have worked together as partners in parenting – it hasn't always been easy, but our children have greatly benefited! ~ Justine Heinsen, Age 59; 2 Children; former Teacher, Community Volunteer

We can form an alliance with other parents and share childcare.

With the shift in America's nuclear families, many children are growing up with only one parent at home. Meeting the needs of one or more children while maintaining a career and a personal life can be daunting. Thinking creatively, asking for help from family and friends, and being open to new friendships with like-minded parents can make all the difference. The adult daughter of a good friend explained her friendship that formed with two other moms when their children were infants. They shifted their schedules to care for each other's children, which not only allowed them to work outside the home, but also formed a new family for them all, providing companionship for both mothers and children. When one of the mothers divorced, these friends were still there for her and her son. They remain close today. ~ Lisa Guy

My parents separated when I was young, and my dad had primary custody. As a fireman, he was called out to fires often in the middle of the night, and my brother and I rode along in his '58 Oldsmobile. He always parked a block or so from the fire, just in case the building exploded. I still clearly remember the way it felt watching him walk away from us, toward that burning structure. . . so worried for his safety, but secure in the knowledge that if anything happened to him, my great aunt would always be there for us. ~ Rick Allen, Father of 1

Lullabies and Song Section 7

Music and song play an important role in many cultures.

They bring us happiness
while encouraging our brains to develop
in the areas of language and reading,
and songs can help our bodies and minds
to work together.

We will listen to music and sing often,
especially during your early years,
helping you to learn the meaning of sounds and words,
and keeping you calm, safe, and enveloped in love.

Shall I sing to you now?

> "To sing is an expression of your being, a being which is becoming.
> ~ Maria Callas, Singer

14

Lullabies and Song

Singing helps form a special bond and creates time to simply "be" together.

Lullabies are simple tunes, sung in a quiet, softly rhythmic voice. The repetitive words and easy, melodic lilt can help to reduce heart and respiration rates and induce a relaxation response in both child and parent, as we sing. It is as if we are both encircled in the softest of cashmere blankets.

Don't be afraid to make up your own lullabies – they can be simple narratives, using the same words you might say out loud. Just repeat those words, over and over again with short lines. It is all about repetition and simplicity. For example:

> *The time has come to go to bed*
> *So settle down and rest your head.*
> *There's nothing else for you to do*
> *Except to know that I love you.*

Switch off all those doubts you may have about not knowing "how" to sing. We can all sing! If you don't have a tune in your head, you can put your own words to a tune you already know, sing a familiar lullaby, or just start singing and see what happens.

Singing to our children helps form a special bond and creates time to simply "be" together. It is a wonderful way to calm and connect, and we can sing any time of the day or night, not just at bedtime!

I can still remember my mum singing lullabies to me as a child, and perhaps you are fortunate enough to have similar memories of your own. Treasure these moments with your little one now. ~ Ruth Baillie; Age 56; Registered Nutrigenomics Counsellor & Nutritional Therapist, Hospice Choir Director

Singing to our children helps calm both parents and little ones alike.

When I'm anxious, I've found that singing to my children helps calm us all – especially if my girls are having a hard time going to sleep. Now I find Penny, my 2-year-old, singing lullabies to her sister and baby dolls. It makes me so happy to see her using this tool to calm herself. Our song is "Baby Mine" by Frank Churchill. Penny asked for it every day for a year, and while I would have preferred to have some variety, the song made her happy, and now it melts my heart when she sings it along with me. I even recorded her singing it in her little 2-year-old voice, so I can remember. . . ~ Courtney Wilcox; Age 33; 2 Children; Stay at Home Mom

Chapter 1

Reflections

Notes for Chapter 1 – Refer back for quick reminders!

Chapter 2

Early Practices – Ways to Ensure Well-Being of Both Baby and Parents

"When you treat children well, they're going to be OK, and if you don't treat them well, they're not going to be OK. It's a very simple message that anybody's great grandmother could have told them. "

~ Gabor Maté, Physician Specializing in Childhood Trauma, Author

Well-Being

Coming home from the hospital with our first child, Kathryn, I experienced a surge of strong emotions. I was relieved – I had survived the birthing process. It had been long, painful, and arduous. After 12 hours of labor, our baby was showing signs of stress, and the doctor was talking about the need for a c-section. Thankfully, Kathryn was born soon after – her face and head a bit distorted from her extended time in the birth canal, but all was well with mother and baby.

At certain points during those early days, I felt overwhelmed – exhausted, with a sense of responsibility so strong that it left me almost paralyzed at times. My parents came to assist for a few days; this helped my husband and me to reset and begin to establish a rhythm of sorts. The next strong emotion was anger – mainly toward my husband. My life – my entire world – had been turned upside down, and his life hadn't seemed to change much at all. He continued going to the office to run our business, and I was home with our tiny baby, feeling tired, isolated, worried, and alone. Looking back, I realize my emotions were out of balance, heightening the effects of new motherhood. My feelings seemed to change minute by minute, and along with the anger came immense love for our daughter, and deep gratitude for the comfortable feel of her steady warmth in my arms.

A friend born in India related that in her culture, new mothers are often cared for by their families and community for at least three months after the birth of their children. They receive daily assistance, and can focus on healing their bodies and bonding with and caring for their newborns. Older women may come regularly to massage mother and baby, and the support provided greatly reduces the postpartum stress and exhaustion which many parents experience with the birth of a child. Numerous cultures throughout the world share similar practices. Unfortunately, many women may feel they are expected to give birth, and soon after, continue on with all of their daily responsibilities while they struggle through the recovery process, breast feeding, sleepless nights and often isolation and loneliness. Understanding this and recognizing ways of supporting new mothers can help to greatly improve those early days.

~ Lisa Guy

Emotions Section 1

Dear one,
It's important to understand that emotions will move through us ~
they come and go, shaping our thoughts and experiences.
One minute we're happy, then sad or angry,
and often these feelings are directed toward those we love.

Let's be careful not to push away or "stuff down" tough emotions.
If we learn to recognize and articulate how we're feeling
we will have greater emotional understanding and well-being.

We can transform uncomfortable emotions
when we address and accept the feelings,
opening space for fond memories and experiences
to gain prominence in our hearts.

Tears are a powerful way to honor our emotions,
and we'll welcome them when they come.

Laughter promotes feelings of happiness,
and we can look for the humor in our lives.

Will you giggle and laugh with me?

> It's the people we love the most who can make us feel the gladdest. . . and the maddest! Love and anger are such a puzzle!
> ~ Mr. Rogers, TV Host, Author

Emotions

 Parents and caregivers who understand their own emotions can teach their children to identify and work through them in a healthy way.

Emotions can have an enormous impact on us, and yet they are often fleeting. Many adults have not learned to be with and experience their own emotions, as they have received little guidance or education in becoming self-aware. Parents and caregivers who understand their own emotions (as well as those of the people around them) and are able to address feelings with appropriate words when needed, can help teach these skills to their children at an early age. This is an ability which has been shown to be strongly tied to successful relationships and overall satisfaction in life ~ Lisa Guy

"Language is our portal to meaning-making, connection, healing, learning, and self-awareness. Having access to the right words can open entire universes." ~ Brené Brown, Atlas of the Heart[1]

 It's important to teach young children how to develop emotional intelligence early on.

For the past twelve years I have worked as a preschool, TK and kindergarten teacher, and I believe that the most important thing to teach young children is how to recognize feelings in themselves and others. Empathy is understanding what someone else is feeling, and giving kids the tools early on to communicate and empathize with others has many benefits.

In my classroom I use a curriculum called Second Step[2], which nurtures children's social and emotional development. This curriculum uses consistent language to explain how a child feels, and how to problem solve, be assertive and communicate with others. We spend time in the classroom reading books that explain feelings and how to manage them. Then we have a discussion and open dialogue afterwards. As the children interact with each other throughout the day, both teachers and students use the language embedded in the curriculum to recognize and address the different feelings and emotions which come forward. In this way the students develop emotional intelligence early on. This knowledge and understanding will serve them well in the future. ~ Brittany Selvy; Age 33; 2 Children; Transitional Kindergarten Teacher

"When parents show they will be anchors even in the storms of emotion that can engulf a child, they convey a message of safety and security: I'll protect you from yourself when you cannot." ~ Abigail Gewirtz, When the World Feels Like a Scary Place[3]

Mental Self-Care Section 2

O h, my love,
Sometimes mothers and fathers can feel overwhelmed
or experience sadness after having a new baby.
We can always reach out for help from our doctor,
family or friends if we need to.

Mindfulness, the practice of paying attention fully
in the present moment,
can help us (both parents and children)
to manage stress, ease tension, and calm strong feelings.

If we choose to use social media, we will use it consciously,
refraining from comparison with others,
and focusing on our many blessings ~
this will help to keep us balanced and grounded.

Let's help each other, shall we?

"Practice being mindful of your breath: Breathing deeply helps us stay present in the moment. Sometimes we don't even realize that we are holding our breath or breathing shallowly, and both can make us feel anxious. Making our exhales longer than our inhales helps us soothe our nervous system, calm down, and think more clearly."
~ Ana O'Sullivan, Family Mental Health Advocate, Mother of 3

Mental Self-Care

 Postpartum depression affects at least 10% of new mothers - help is available.

Although many women have little difficulty with being a new mother or adding a new member to the family, this is not always the case. PMAD (perinatal mood and anxiety disorders) are the most common complication of pregnancy, affecting at least 10% of women. If you find that you are overwhelmed or are having difficulty adjusting to your new situation, you are not alone. Speak up and seek help. Prior to being sent home from the hospital you should be assessed for PMAD, and your pediatrician should be assessing this as well. The most commonly used assessment tool is the Edinburgh Postnatal Depression Scale (EPDS). It is important to know that symptoms can appear any time during pregnancy and the first 12 months after childbirth. The best thing you can do for you, your family, and your children is to seek help through your healthcare provider, or community/online resources.[4] ~ Anonymous Women's Health Specialist.

Postpartum Support International (PSI): https://www.postpartum.net.

"New mothers should be aware that some changes can be expected after childbirth, which are not considered postpartum depression. These changes may include fatigue, difficulty sleeping, poor appetite, and low libido. If these changes seem more than expected by you or a loved one, an evaluation for PMAD should be done by your healthcare professional." ~ Megan Guy, MD

 Parents and caregivers can maintain a healthy balance by consciously using only the good elements of social media.

As a new mom, I know I must take care of my own mental well-being, so I can be the parent I want to be. I've learned that social media can be hard on my mental outlook, as it contains a plethora of images, portraying the "perfect" lives of so many people. What I've come to find is that the power resides within me. I can use social media for positive purposes, including quick parenting tips (from credible sources), cleaning hacks, recipes, at home preschool activities, and so much more. Social media can also be a great source of connection, and sometimes even advice. On the downside, I am aware that it can lead to comparison, self-doubt, and an unrelenting fear of the "mom guilt" of not doing enough. In reality, perfect children, perfect husbands, perfect vacations, and perfect lives do not exist. I know that trying to keep up with the images portrayed on a screen by social media can only lead to anxiety, depression, and an overall unhappiness with my own life and family. I have been able to maintain a healthy balance by consciously using only the good elements of social media. I "unfollow" what doesn't serve me, refrain from comparing my home, family, and possessions to those of others, focus on daily gratitude for my many blessings, and follow only those accounts which align with my interests and parenting style. ~ Brittany Selvy; Age 33; 2 Children; Transitional Kindergarten Teacher

Physical Self-Care of New Mothers Section 3

Carrying and giving birth to you
was an incredible experience.
Now that you are here,
I know it is important to continue to take care of myself.

I'll do my best to stay hydrated,
eat well, and exercise carefully.
This will help me to heal, replenish my energy,
and regain my strength.

My body has changed
with the miracle of carrying you.

I know I must be kind and patient with myself.

"It took your body 9 months, plus labor and delivery
to get here – give your body a year to recover."
~ Wendy Shaw Dahl, MPT, Mother of 1

Physical Self-Care of New Mothers

Recovery after pregnancy and childbirth can be more difficult than many people realize.

After a relatively speedy and painless delivery, I thought the most difficult part of my pregnancy was behind me – I had delivered my daughter and expected to be back to normal within a week. Little did I know, the hardest part of my journey was just beginning. Three days after delivery we went out for a walk – I felt incredibly weak, and everything hurt. I was so disappointed in myself, thinking, "I'm supposed to be tougher than this."

I absolutely wasn't prepared for the next two weeks – it hurt to stand up, sit down, walk, pee, cough, sneeze, laugh, and simply live my life. I had underestimated the recovery process! I had a minor tear that required stitches as well as what the doctor described as a rug-burn-like-mark – nothing major. . . How could so many women have gone through this before me and never said anything about it? ~ Abrianna Rose; Age 29; 1 Child; Sales Manager

New mothers should plan for a year of recovery after childbirth – taking care to eat well, hydrate, exercise, prioritize sleep, take personal moments, and refrain from dieting.

Congratulations – your body has accomplished a physical miracle! Now it needs recovery, which is just as important as activity. You are literally rebuilding your body and brain on the cellular level. To feel like yourself again, your body needs deep sleep, nourishing food, and nurturing thoughts. Give your body a year – it took almost a year to get here, and it will take that long or longer to fully recover.

The exciting first year for the baby is also the postpartum year for rebuilding the mother's body. Adequate sleep and nutrition are often hard to come by. Sleep is when we heal – grab any chance to sleep or nap that you can. Feeding yourself whole foods, fresh vegetables and fruit, and drinking plenty of fresh water will replenish your cells while enriching your milk for the baby. Our bodies need additional calories when breastfeeding, and healing from stitches or surgery. Please ignore images from the media. This is no time to diet. It's also not the time for fast food, junk food, or fad diets. Whatever you eat is what your body will use to rebuild your cells.

The quality of our recovery after having a baby with proper rest, nutrition, and emotional care, determines the quality of our life in later years. If we can facilitate the best recovery after each baby, we have the power to avoid problems in the future including pelvic floor issues, osteoporosis, back pain, and core instability. ~ Wendy Shaw Dahl; Age 53; 1 Child; Founder/ MPT, Mamamorphosis Physical Therapy for Moms

Parents Nurturing Their Own Interests and Talents

Section 4

Little one, a sense of purpose
brings greater satisfaction in life.

Learning new skills,
having unusual experiences,
and working toward specific goals
all help to bring fulfillment and joy.

When time allows
we will do our best to explore our own interests and talents,
showing you that continuing to grow as individuals,
even once we've reached adulthood,
brings contentment and gratitude to our lives.

We know we will have more patience,
more enthusiasm,
and be a better parent
if we challenge ourselves,
pursue our interests,
and make a meaningful difference in this world.

Where will your interests be drawn?

"All people want to be known and valued for their knowledge and skills. They want their talents to matter." ~ Don Maruska, Take Charge of Your Talents

Parents Nurturing Their Own Interests and Talents

I've been interested in music for most of my life. Now that I am a high school science teacher with a wife and two children, my time is limited, but I still make a point of carving away a little time to play my bass, and sometimes I can even convince my wife to join me on the drums. . . Our kids benefit as well -- making and enjoying music together is the greatest!
~ Anthony Porchia, Father of 2

New parents can benefit from continued involvement in adult pursuits or interests.

The times when I was least satisfied with being a mother are still clear in my mind. They were always the situations when I felt cut off from adult pursuits or adult stimulation in the company of others. Much of this was due to our frequent moves of brief duration for my husband's job. It was wonderful to be in Salt Lake City for a whole year, so I could make friends, volunteer, and learn to ski. Living in Shaker Heights for 7 years allowed me to help start a babysitting co-op and take an active role in The League of Women Voters and PTA. At this point I was home raising our three children, but these and other activities kept me fulfilled beyond the routines of mothering. ~Rita Mathern; Age 77; 4 Children; Past English Teacher/Mentor/Community Volunteer

"My advice to new mothers is: "Don't lose yourself in motherhood. Keep the flame alive for your own personal goals, or your daughters won't know how." ~ Carol Paquet; 3 Children;
Multi Media Visual Artis

Take care not to lose yourself in motherhood.

I tend to give all I've got to my children. My partner has been helping me to understand that it's okay for the two of us to go out to dinner alone once in a while. I don't need to feel guilty -- it's not necessary for the kids to be with us every second. In the past, I always made sure that everyone in the family was served their food first, and often I would sit down later to a cold meal. If my teenage son asked to have my special Starbucks drink, I would hand it over to him without a second thought – and when I went to shop for clothes, I would forgo something I needed for clothing my kids didn't really even need or want. I am realizing how important it is for my kids to understand that I have desires, interests, and feelings too! I'm learning how to advocate for myself. It's good for my kids to think of me as a human being who deserves respect, not just someone there to take care of them. ~ Maribel Perez; Age 32; 4 Kids; House-cleaner

Friends and Companionship Section 5

Life is always better with friends!

We will join a class or group,
share our stories
and connect with others.

Won't this be so much fun?

"Find a group of people who
challenge and inspire you;
spend a lot of time with them,
and it will change your life.
~ Amy Poehler, Actress, Writer, Producer

Friends and Companionship

Knowing how important friendships will be for this next part of my journey, I've spent some time investigating a new online app, designed to help new moms connect in the real world. It's been so fun meeting other women who are in a similar stage of life, and I was happy to have two of them attend my recent baby shower, along with their little ones. My baby is due in two months, and we already have a welcoming community to be a part of. ~ Christiana Magneson, Age 33

Healthy relationships will allow both parents and little ones to thrive!

When I reflect back on my early years of parenting, I realize that there were things I could have done to make this period of my life easier, as well as more rewarding and enjoyable. Most likely driven by my personality, I was always a bit hard on myself, usually expecting perfection, and I tended not to reach out much for help or companionship. When I didn't do things "just right" I was embarrassed, and the last thing I wanted to do was share this information with others.

Watching my own daughter go through her early parenting years, I was delighted to see her with her new-mother friends, laughing and joking about the things going wrong in their lives, and sharing stories of the trials and tribulations of raising little ones. Their happy, carefree attitude, desire to support one another, and comfortable companionship made me smile every time.

Fast friendships often form during challenging times, and the early years of parenthood can be much more rewarding when shared with those who align with our outlook, energy, and goals. It is such a benefit to engage with positive people, as the relationships we choose to be a part of will directly impact how quickly we grow. ~ Martha Chivens; Age 78; 3 Children; 7 Grandchildren; Former Preschool Founder/Director

"Throughout life, we all experience struggles of one kind or another, and having supportive friends can make all the difference. Many people choose to tackle hardships on their own, but having someone to lean on, ask advice of, and receive comfort and support from is truly a gift." ~ Kerri Mahoney, Mother of 3

Looking on the Bright Side Section 6

Oh, my love ~
life is fluid, dynamic, and constantly changing,
and our daily attitude
profoundly affects the experiences we have.

It is so important to look at things clearly
in an affirmative light
and count our many blessings each day.

To be alive is a precious gift,
and we will make a regular practice
of recognizing and expressing our gratitude.

What are you most thankful for?

66 Train your mind
to see the good in
every situation. 99
~ Unknown

Looking on the Bright Side

I was 5 years old when I realized I could choose happiness over sadness. With a mother who suffered from mental illness, it was hard to know how she would be feeling from day-to-day, and how she would relate to me and my siblings. I think I developed an outlook of gratitude early on, along with the knowledge that we can all make a conscious decision to look for the good in life and begin every day with a positive attitude. As I learned when I was small, it's just so much more fun to be happy. ~ Jasi Sotello, Mother of 4

☆   ☆   ☆

Conveying positivity and happiness will make a lasting impact on our families.

My mother was an eternal optimist! In 1943, before the advent of sonograms, she was quite surprised when she arrived at the hospital and gave birth to two children instead of one. The fall and winter after my sister and I were born, it rained and rained in Pasadena. Our older brother was 2 ½ and still in diapers, and Dad strung several clothes lines across our living room to accommodate the laundry for all three of us. Later on, when Mom talked about those hectic days, I could feel her happiness and joy. She and my father had married late in life and were so grateful to have children. She never complained about the amount of work, number of diapers, or the chaotic nature of that time.

In 1969, before our first son was born, my husband, Don, constructed a clothesline in the backyard of our Arizona home. Mom came from Oregon to help us, although she was quite weak from cancer. Don insisted on hanging up the cloth diapers himself when he returned home from work. One evening, when he was outside, I could see Mom was crying. "I wish I were strong enough to hang the diapers," she told me. "Oh, but you were so strong, and you hung up so many. . . remember?" I replied. But I knew how she was feeling.

I so appreciate the example Mom set when she joked with Dad about the "beautiful" clotheslines strung across our living room, and wanted to help so badly when she was very ill. I can still feel the positivity and happiness that radiated from her, and throughout my life, I have continued to do my best to carry it forward. ~ Martha Chivens; Age 78; 3 Children; 7 Grandchildren; Former Preschool Founder/Director

☆   ☆   ☆

"Since my kids were young, I've always tried to live each day as if it's the last, and make simple, ordinary days feel special. I like to encourage new mothers to pull out their grandmother's china, teach their young ones to fold a cloth napkin, and make a macaroni and cheese dinner into an elegant feast!" ~ Susie Kenny, Mother of 8

Significance of Smiling Section 7

Never underestimate the power of a smile.
It can brighten someone's day
bring us a new friend,
and relay hope, kindness, and love.

Little one, you make me smile!

"Too often we underestimate the power of a touch, a smile, a kind word, a listening ear, an honest compliment, or the smallest act of caring, all of which have the potential to turn a life around."
~ Leo Buscaglia, Author

Significance of Smiling

For years I've been volunteering in our schools on the Central Coast and taking note of the students I pass in halls and on the school grounds. From the time I was a young child, I've always greeted those passing by with a smile and nod. It's been enlightening to note that most younger children are interested in new people and eager to connect with a smile or word, while preteens and teens seem to become increasingly less interested. As parents, we can model intentional smiling in our everyday interactions - especially with our own children - and likely reap the benefits of boosting our own mood and the mood of those around us!

~ Lisa Guy

Modeling smiling to our children on a regular basis will have a lasting positive effect.

My mother came to the U.S. from China at age 40, with no formal education and speaking no English. Consequently, she lacked self-assurance, preferring to stay hidden from society, and made contact with only a small group of Chinese-speaking locals. As a result, I too lacked any semblance of confidence and was especially shy. It wasn't until I started a job with a cosmetics company while in college that belief in myself began to emerge. This is when I discovered the magic of a simple smile. Regardless of how scared or nervous I felt inside, if I genuinely smiled, made direct eye contact and acknowledged another, a sort of magic happened for both myself and the recipient of the smile.

When our daughter Tia was young, I took her everywhere with me, holding her in my arms so she could see what I saw. I would chat with her before entering the post office, bank or grocery store, encouraging her to look at the faces of the workers and notice their expressions. If they appeared bored or disengaged, we would do our best to make them smile.

All it took was smiling big ourselves, acknowledging the worker, and engaging in small conversation outside their normal interactions: "How is your day going today?" or "You are really efficient in what you do!" Every time, we would see them smile in a way that showed us they felt seen and valued. I am sure that by modeling smiling on a regular basis, we can help our children learn the beneficial habit of smiling and interacting positively with others.

Now Tia is grown up and is a genuine "smiler!" She makes an effort to connect with those who cross her path, letting them know they are important, and they matter. There is power in smiling, and when we smile to our children and others, they are in turn, empowered as well."

~ Carol Gin; 60+ years old; 4 children, 1 grandchild; cosmetics company Director

Chapter 2
Reflections

Notes for Chapter 2 – Refer back for quick reminders!

Chapter 3

Authoritative (or Heart-Centered) Parenting –
Ongoing Communication and Good Habits
Work Together to Foster Healthy,
Well-Balanced Children

"Day by day, what you choose, what you think, and what you do is who you become."

~ Heraclitus, Greek Philosopher

Habits

The activities we spend our time on can inspire growth or limit our interests and potential.

I am grateful for the good habits my parents helped me establish early on, including the desire to treat people well and always try my best, a love of reading, and an appreciation of nature. They also taught me self-discipline; I enjoy working hard to accomplish a goal and rewarding myself afterwards.

I spent 2 ½ hours each evening putting our five little ones to bed. I started with the youngest – we would snuggle while reading a story, then talk for a bit about the day's events and end with a song. This was our opportunity to discuss the events of the day or concerns they might have, just between the two of us.

The activities we spend our time on can inspire growth or limit our interests and potential. Before our son William was born, my husband told me he didn't want William playing video games. He was determined to keep him from establishing the habit of using technology early on, as this would likely form an addiction, and limit the time he had for trying new things. Initially I was concerned about how this would affect his friendships. As it was, our son did miss out on some playdates, but the friends he had understood our rules. They had a great time playing outside, building Legos, learning new board games, and as they grew older, playing music and sports together. ~ Lisa Guy

Modeling exercise and leading an active life will help to develop beneficial habits in our children.

As a physical therapist who works with patients of all ages, I have seen firsthand the benefits of leading an active life. I have also seen the impact adults can have on their children in terms of views on exercise. My own love for physical activity sprang from a love for athletics and movement as a kid. Luckily, my parents encouraged outdoor fun and participation in sports; they also let my wild siblings and me work out our energy despite the chaos it sometimes caused. However, when I became a teenager and had a break from organized sports I was not sure how to exercise or how to be active on my own. My dad gifted me an exercise book for teenagers which changed my life, providing me with tools to explore fitness on my own. This started my journey as a lifelong athlete, learner, and movement specialist. The benefits of physical activity are numerous. When active, our bodies learn how to heal, recover from injury, cope when uncomfortable, and grow resilient. I believe that exercise is for everyone, and it is easiest to form as a life habit when taught at a young age. ~ Kathryn Guy-Paterson; Age 32; MPT

"Good habits formed at youth make all the difference." ~ Aristotle, Greek Philosopher

Deep Responsibility of New Parents Section 1

Dear child, we are excited to watch your gifts develop,
and understand the responsibility we carry as your parents.

As you grow,
together we will explore your strengths, interests, and aptitudes,
learn how to set and work toward goals,
establish good habits,
and nurture and empower you to be all you can be.

What amazing things will you do with your life?

*"We may soon realize that being a parent is MUCH harder than anyone led us to believe…
whether it's our first or our third, we're doing it ALL for the first time. We will naturally make
mistakes and need to remember that this is a part of the human experience. Caring for our
needs and being present for those we love are the greatest gifts we can give to our babies
and families."* ~ Ana O'Sullivan, Family Mental Health Advocate, Mother of 3

Deep Responsibility of New Parents

"The day you found out that you would have a child, you enrolled for full-time service. Your contract called for a minimum of eighteen years of service with an understanding that you would be on 'active reserve' for several years after that." ~ Gary Chapman and Ross Campbell, The 5 Love Languages of Children.[1]

Parenthood, like life, is a marathon rather than a sprint.

As we enter adulthood, we may long for simpler, more carefree days, but that doesn't mean we are unhappy. We assume more responsibility, which seems to double (perhaps with each child) during the "parenting period" of our lives. With more commitments, and less free time and flexibility, we may feel a range of emotions, including grief. Bringing a new baby into this world presents unique challenges requiring mental strength, adaptation, and adjustment. We must forgive ourselves for all of the emotions, even the negative ones, that may come up along our parenting journey. They are normal and healthy! What we're doing is difficult, very important, and requires humility, and acceptance of both ourselves and our feelings. Having the endurance, positive outlook, and patience we'd like to have every day of our journey is not possible. Even so, understanding that each day gives us the opportunity to do our best, helps us to be resilient, and to learn and grow as parents. ~ Molly ZagRodny ; Age 53; 2 Children; Mission Director, Faculty Commons, a Ministry of Cru

"Parents should realize that some of the things they say to their children will be remembered forever . . .

. . . whether good or bad, positive or negative. It's hard to know which words will 'stick,' so be thoughtful about the things you say and the way you speak." ~ Aurelia Guy, Daughter, Age 25

Sensitive and responsive caregivers provide an environment rich in growth experiences.

"Serve and return" is not only a concept in paddle sports, but it's a vital element in childhood development. A baby's cries, gestures, or coos are her "serves." Perhaps she cries for a diaper change, reaches out for a hug, or coos her contentment. Then as parents and caregivers return the baby's serve with a loving response and continue this back-and-forth exchange, they are helping her feel connected and loved, forming a secure attachment, and at the same time helping to build the baby's neural connections and strengthen her developing brain. ~ Nadine McCarty; 64; 2 Children; retired Parent Education Instructor

Formation of Habits Section 2

Did you know,
habits form the basis of our existence?
They can be the making or undoing of us.

Bad habits are easy to establish
and hard to break.

We will work together to build good habits
from the beginning
which will benefit you for the rest of your life.

If we find a habit or practice no longer serves us,
we will work to make the necessary changes or adjustments.

Will you help me, as I help you?

" Just one time without
correction, and an action can
become a habit. It's so important
to stop negative behaviors
before they become routine! "
~ Nina Truch, Mother of 2

Formation of Habits

"The only thing you absolutely have to know, is the location of the library." ~ Albert Einstein, Theoretical Physicist

One of the very best things we can do for our children is to instill the habit and love of reading!

In my family, reading has been a priority since I can remember. Television time was limited, and from an early age, my four siblings and I were always encouraged to read. My mom read us stories and books every night until we were reading proficiently on our own, and then my dad read some of the same books we did, so we could talk about the stories and characters when we were finished. Reading for fun from a young age (in addition to required schoolwork) has deeply benefited me throughout my academic, professional, and personal life. Reading comprehension and speed are often cited as the core benefits of reading, but I've found the less obvious rewards to outweigh the traditional in my life.

As a preteen I became very interested in fantasy books and loved stepping into a world of wonder and imagination for a while, leaving my normal, everyday life behind. I find it interesting that reading fantasy stories about wizards all those years ago was, in fact, preparing me for school exams over a decade later. I'd call it almost magical! Apologies for the terrible pun. As a disclaimer, reading has not been shown to improve poor senses of humor.

Reading avidly throughout my adolescence has helped me in many ways! My interest and aptitude for proper grammar solidified in 8th grade and has helped with both course work and school exams, as well as standardized testing. I also realize that our world is filled with constant dopamine rushes and instant gratification (thanks to TV, social media, and video games), but books have given me a slower form of gratification. I believe they have taught me patience for more complex work and relationships down the road.

Now that I am out of school and pursuing my career in the field of Tech, I realize what an important role writing plays in almost every industry in today's world. Whether it's a tradesman who writes emails to prospective clients, a retail worker who writes a cover letter application to a local store, or an engineer who articulates the benefits of their recent invention, the written word is the conduit to express ourselves. The ability to communicate eloquently and succinctly pays dividends in every workplace, and this is a skill learned over time by reading. ~ Maliena Guy; Age 28; Product Manager

"Good habits are like muscle memory – you don't even have to think about them, and they automatically help you work toward your goals." ~ Janet Crabb, Mother of 3

Being Present Section 3

So many things in life call for our attention
but now that you are here
we will do our best to be genuinely present,
making the most of our time together.

Can you feel my awareness and love?

"Be in the moment and use your breathing to help you stay grounded. When we are fully present (not thinking about the past or future), we are better able to learn about our baby. Use your senses to soak in the memories – when it's bath time, focus on the richness of bath time fun... the sounds, smells, and touch. There's nothing cuter than a clean, content baby in pj's!" ~ Ana O'Sullivan, Family Mental Health Advocate, Mother of 3

Being Present

Our children benefit when we are present and spend intentional time with them.

My birth mom, who was a single parent, passed away when I was 14 years old. A few years later, my best friend's family adopted me. I have had the honor and blessing of having two incredible moms, and thinking of them, I'm consumed by an overwhelming feeling of love. I've wanted to be a mom since childhood and have always loved working with children. For the past four years I have taught preschool and kindergarten students who are deaf or hearing impaired. My education and experience have solidified my understanding of child development, especially language acquisition, but becoming a mom taught me things I had never learned before. When thinking of the childhood I want my 2-year-old daughter to have, most of all it is for her to experience that same overall feeling of love I've had for my two moms.

Important moments occur while life is happening. As a full-time working mom, it's essential that I'm intentional about being present when I get to be with my daughter. I've come to realize that she doesn't need me to design elaborate activities every day or buy her the fanciest toys, I just need to sit and play and read and bring her alongside me in all that I am doing. Early language acquisition is a specialty of mine, and I've been delighted to see her language grow from simple activities like reading, singing, and talking about the world around us.

I've also learned that caring for myself is an important part of being the best mom I can be. Date nights with my husband and girls' lunches with my friends are good things, not something to feel guilt over. As parents, we all have different backgrounds, education, passions and experiences. Parenting will be unique for us all, and will foster our own growth in amazing ways. ~ Destinee Glasser; Age 28; 1 Child; Preschool/Kindergarten Teacher for Deaf and Hard of Hearing

When we're feeling out of sorts, "5 Senses Breathing[2]" can help to ground us and bring us back to the present.

Wherever I am, in nature or just sitting in a room, I pick one of the 5 senses and focus on it while breathing deeply. If that sense is sight, I open my eyes wide and take in everything around me – the colors, shapes, objects, plants, flowers, animals. . . I truly see them, name them, and take a deep, cleansing breath. Then I move to hearing. I close my eyes, take a deep breath, and listen to the myriad sounds – the ticking of a clock, the rustling of branches moving in the wind, the crunch of my feet on the ground. My sense of touch might be feeling the warmth of the sun on my face... I use my 5 fingers to remember each sense, remembering to belly breathe between each finger. If I lose focus or have a distracting thought, I am gentle with myself and return to the first finger, the first sense and just breathe . . . we can teach this to our children. ~ Elise Thompson, LMFT, Mother of 2

Starting and Ending the Day Right Section 4

Creating morning and evening rituals
will help us begin and end each day
in a constructive way…naturally, intentionally,
and in alignment with our goals and values.

We may choose to write short messages,
affirmations or mantras,
placing them in select locations throughout our home.

These gentle reminders can give us courage and motivation
as they help to reinforce ideas and perspectives we wish to cultivate.

Where shall we begin?

"My morning and evening rituals probably have the biggest effect on how I show up as a parent. It's not strict, but it's fairly consistent most days. It helps me be intentional about how I live each day, rather than reacting to what life throws at me."
~ Simone Davies, The Montessori Toddler[3]

Starting and Ending the Day Right

If we begin and end each day well, the middle will likely follow along the same path.

Our boys are almost 6 and 7 years old, and from early on we've made a point of giving special attention to beginning and ending each day in a certain way. If I can wake up 30 minutes or so before the rest of my family, I can ease gracefully into the day. Sipping on a cup of tea or coffee while reflecting on the events of the coming hours gives me the solitude to ground myself before the business of the day begins. I imagine those who enjoy quiet time at night can find the same benefit once the kids are in bed. We parents must care for ourselves first and foremost so that we may be fortified and ready to give what we can to our children!

As my children grow and move from one stage to the next, I realize I must be flexible! My older son, Parker, now often wakes before 5:30 a.m., which makes it challenging to rise before him. Knowing that this is likely a phase we will be moving through helps keep my perspective in check and my thinking positive.

The end of our day is a time we all look forward to. From the beginning, my husband and I read books to Parker – even while he was still in the womb. We make adjustments as the boys grow, and now my husband reads chapter books with Parker in bed, while Mason and I read and talk in the living room. When they're ready, the "big" boys call us into the bedroom, and I climb into the bottom bunk with Mason to sing the songs they both request. Between songs we switch places, so each boy has a chance to be with us both. It's a beautiful time of bonding for the four of us, and the boys drift off to sleep in a relaxed and happy state. I'm not sure how long this will continue, but I know the time is finite and this makes it all the more precious. ~ Jenn Hoff; Age 43, 2 Children; Elementary School Teacher/Health & Wellness Coach

We can give ourselves daily encouragement with short messages posted around the home.

I had a special way of motivating and encouraging myself when my children were young. It began with stepping back and thinking about the things I really believed to be important, and from this exercise I created little messages and mantras, which I positioned in various places around the house. When I awoke in the wee hours of the morning to a crying baby, I took a few seconds to breathe and repeat a mantra – something like: "I will be patient - sleepless nights are only temporary." ~ Janice Selvy, Mother of 2

Disentangling from a Negative Storyline Section 5

L ittle one,
we have the power within us to be at peace.

We can step back from our thoughts,
and refrain from fabricating negative stories in our minds.
Misunderstandings and pain
can come from assuming we know what another is thinking.

Emotions can arise from past experiences.
Connected memories or patterns can return, time and again,
bringing with them unpleasant feelings and reactions.
Understanding this can help us to keep from attaching an old story
to a new experience.

When our emotions become heightened
we can get in touch with our bodies through our breath,
breathing slowly and deeply, in and out ~
aware that our words and story can create discord or peace.
Disentangling from a negative storyline brings calm and clarity.

We know you will be watching us closely,
and learning from our actions.

Let's keep our stories positive – they have the power to heal!

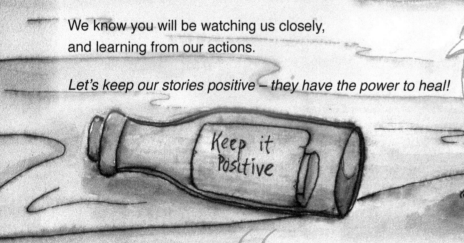

Keep it Positive

"It's not always possible to do away with negative thinking, but with persistence and practice, one can gain mastery over our thoughts so they do not take the upper hand."
~ Stephen Richards, New Zealand-Australian Racing Driver

Disentangling from a Negative Storyline

"It doesn't make sense to imagine we know what another is thinking . . .

. . . the imagining is so often negative! Asking others what is on their mind, listening carefully, and understanding that they may have thoughts and outlooks which I may never fully understand, has proved beneficial time and again." ~ Lisa Guy

Reframe your story – relate to everything in your life as something that enables growth.

Your mental attitude is the only thing over which you, and you alone, have complete control. Every adversity, sorrow, or defeat, whether or not you caused it to happen, contains the seed of an equivalent benefit or opportunity. When you fall into a negative mindset, with thoughts of fear, anger, and frustration, your mind will only draw these same things to you. Reframe your thinking. When you adopt a beneficial mental attitude, your confidence in yourself (and others) will guide you toward beneficial outcomes in your life. You make the choice. You shape your own destiny.

Reframe your story. Relate to every circumstance in your life as something that enables growth. It may be that your saddest experience will bring your greatest benefits. My older brother was born with Down syndrome. My mother taught us to regard him as the family's greatest gift, as so he was. He taught us unconditional love. He was our compassion teacher, our soft pillow in the night. We saw him as the bringer of joy into our world, and he was loved by all.

My mother's creative vision ensured that what could have been a challenge, limitation or handicap in our lives has remained to this day, one of the happiest experiences of my life. It also taught me how to approach my thoughts - to be the master, not the slave, of my resulting emotions. I learned that whatever I think today becomes what I am tomorrow. This is the essence of the power of a positive mental attitude and of constantly cultivating a positive storyline. My mother's vision has fostered my imagination and continues to inspire me with enthusiasm that makes all of the work in my life a labor of love. ~ Hilary Anderson; Age 66; Teacher/Coach/Licensed Spiritual Healer

"Emotions stay on and on when we fuel them with words . . .

. . . It's like pouring kerosene on an ember to make it blaze. Without words, without the repetitive thoughts, the emotions don't last longer than one and a half minutes."
~ Pema Chödrön, <u>Living Beautifully</u>[4]

Cultivating Cooperation Section 6

My dearest,
understanding that you are a unique individual
with your own thoughts, desires, and will
is of the utmost importance.

As you grow,
we will make a habit of viewing the challenges we encounter
as teaching and learning opportunities for us both.

To best accomplish this,
we will need a foundation of connection and trust.
This begins with accepting you for who you are
and making sure you feel a strong sense
of belonging and significance.

Modeling asking for feedback and receiving it
without being defensive or pointing blame
will help to shape your view of what's possible
and assist in your quest to find your place in the world.

Do you know how much I love you?

> I've found I can encourage cooperation if my requests are tied to fun, and when trying to move the kids quickly toward the car, we often 'fly,' 'skip,' or 'hop' our way there.
>
> ~Amanda Ferrell, Mother of 2

Cultivating Cooperation

Parents and caregivers can shape the skills needed to give and receive feedback.

Children are constantly receiving feedback from their environments and learning from it. A child takes her first step and the adults in the room smile, applaud, and encourage. So, she tries it again and again, looking around for the reaction. A child touches something hot and he feels the burn. He doesn't touch it again. Both of these scenarios show the significance of feedback.

As a child's ability to process and integrate the spoken word expands, so too does the need for more sophisticated feedback. Healthy feedback broadens a child's view of what is possible and helps clarify his or her unique strengths, talents, and value in relation to the world. As part of our daily interactions, parents and caregivers can shape the skills needed to give and receive feedback. When you model asking for feedback and receive it without being defensive or blaming, your child will begin to emulate your actions.

(Example):

(Parent) "I want to see if I can do a better job of getting you to school on time each day. What do you think I could do differently in the morning that will help us both get ready on time?"

The incredibly tricky but essential piece is to listen, affirm, and avoid defending, justifying or blaming.

(Child) "Stop looking at your phone when I'm getting ready."

While you could be doing something essential on your phone, if you defend or justify, you will be signaling that their feedback is not valued. Instead, affirm and become curious.

(Parent) "Thank you. I hear you. Can you say a little more about how that would help?"

(Child) "I need to ask you questions and you keep telling me to wait. I can't get ready until you answer me."

Now, together you can create a solution. When your child discloses preferences, challenges and changes, respond by identifying the action as feedback.

(Parent) "Oh, thank you for that feedback. This helps me to understand."

~ Beth Wonson; Age 63; 2 Children; 5 Grandchildren; Executive Coach/Author/Speaker

☆   ☆   ☆

"The secret to enlisting our children's cooperation is the same for all aspects of successful parenting: respect. Newborns, infants, toddlers, and preschoolers – people of all ages – want to be engaged with, included and invited to participate rather than have things done to them." ~ Janet Lansbury, No Bad Kids[5]

Anticipation and Prevention Section 7

Little one, throughout your life, you will encounter challenges ~
one after the next.
The way you face these challenges will define you as a person.

As you grow, we will help you see
that your actions and the decisions you make,
lead to consequences which will profoundly affect your life.

We will guide you, making a habit of listening actively
and encouraging you to speak freely ~
posing questions which help you to recognize and trust your intuition,
while building confidence in yourself.

We will do our best to help you
to anticipate potential dangers and unsafe situations,
think through big decisions,
and develop your critical reasoning skills.
Mistakes will happen along the way,
but our ongoing communication will assist in your growth,
and likely save you from unpleasant outcomes.

Will you be open and accepting as we share our knowledge
and wisdom with awareness and love?

CADTMP

"Parenting involves
thousands upon thousands
of conversations, in widely
different circumstances,
across every age from a
child's birth through
adulthood.

~ Abigail Gerwitz, When
the World Feels Like a
Scary Place[6]

46

Anticipation and Prevention

New parents, please be aware of the powerful influence you have on your child. You will be watched and imitated! Your influence will be especially relevant when the subjects of alcohol/drug use and sexual exploration arise in later years. If you educate yourself and your child early on (while you have the greatest influence) and are careful to set a good example, your child's healthy, successful development is likely to be the reward. ~ Lisa Guy

It's important to educate children early, talk to them often, be knowledgeable of their activities, and always shower them with love.

As the President of the non-profit POSAFY[7] (Prevention of Substance Abuse for Youth) I know first-hand that we must educate our children on the harms of substance abuse at an early age. Kids are unlikely to listen once they are in their pre-teens and onward, but they will be receptive during their early life developmental stages. We can give them a chance, so that when they are confronted with peer pressure, anxiety or depression, they have the appropriate knowledge and tools to manage. The temptation to use drugs to satisfy the need to belong, the desire to self-medicate, or simply wanting to experience something new, must be met with a strong, inner understanding of the negative outcomes that accompany the use of drugs.

With the proliferation and acceptance of marijuana use today, the need to educate is greater than ever. Today's marijuana is much stronger than it was in the past. This increased potency, along with the belief that it is harmless (and even beneficial), is causing an avalanche of issues with our youth. Many young people are experiencing a variety of dangerous and unpleasant outcomes including anxiety and depression due to marijuana use. A gateway drug is any first drug used that opens the pleasure center of the brain and primes it for addiction. Whether a youth is predisposed due to mental health genetics or has other triggers, using marijuana, alcohol or prescription drugs will have a negative effect on the underdeveloped brain. Educating our children on the dangers, and empowering them to make healthy choices, will help them do better. ~ Jody Belsher; 3 Children; 6 Grandchildren; President POSAFY/MA in Addiction Studies

"Parents can teach young children about the privacy of body parts, and that no one has the right to touch their bodies if they don't want that to happen. Children should also learn to respect the right to privacy of other people." ~ HealthyChildren.org

Balancing Technology Section 8

Did you know,
you will learn language best
from personal relationships?
We will provide you with many
real-life opportunities,
especially during your first five years.

Rather than using electronics
to help calm or entertain you,
we will do our best
to set up a safe and interesting
play environment at home,
take you on walks,
read you books,
plan fun and interesting activities,
talk and sing with you,
and allow for quiet and contemplative time.

Doesn't this sound delightful?

66 Addressing technology early on with our
children is so much easier than trying to 99
remove, limit, or corral it later!
~ Rachel Kovesdi, Mother of 2

Balancing Technology

"Children younger than two years need hands-on exploration and social interaction with trusted caregivers to develop their cognitive, language, motor and social-emotional skills... Parents' background television use distracts from parent-child interactions and child play. Heavy parent use of mobile devices is associated with fewer verbal and nonverbal interactions between parents and children and may be associated with more parent-child conflict. Because parent media use is a strong predictor of child media habits, reducing parental media use and enhancing parent-child interactions may be an important area of behavior change." ~ Policy Statement, American Academy of Pediatrics, Media and Young Minds, 2016[8]

If handled appropriately, technology can be beneficial for the social, emotional, and intellectual development of our young people.

Access to technology has changed the educational landscape, and we as parents and educators need to work together with students to adapt in constructive ways! As a parent, I have given a great deal of thought to technology and the digital world, and I realize that if handled appropriately, technology can be beneficial rather than detrimental to the development of our young people.

My own kids are learning and interacting with the greater world through technology. Daughter Charlotte spends time looking at design websites which excite and inspire her. Son Griffin has an affinity for photography, music, and surfing and uses the internet to explore those interests.

It's important to connect with our children about what they're looking at when on social media – ask them to see what they think is funny. . . what they're interested in. Today's parents need to be informed, involved, and in charge. Our children are counting on us to guide them through their early years! When a child is provided with a cell phone, it's helpful to establish certain ground rules and ensure they are consistently followed. We have made mealtime sacred and phone-free from the start. Movie night has been a favorite shared family experience we all look forward to.

We ourselves use technology, and our children watch us closely. We've found it works well to assist them early on by controlling their use of technology, then moving to shared control as they get older, and ultimately, when they are ready, passing the control over to them with increased responsibility, but continuing to have an active interest in their pastimes. ~ Jen Sawyer; Age 48; 3 Children; Library/Media Tech

Discipline Section 9

Dear child, from the very beginning
may we view discipline as an opportunity to teach,
stay calm and grounded,
and provide you with a solid foundation
as you learn to interact with others,
foster and maintain healthy relationships,
and thrive in our society.

While learning valuable skills
and recognizing the consequences of your actions,
you'll begin to experience the many benefits
of clear boundaries and expectations:
an increased capacity for self-control,
the freedom to safely learn and explore your environment,
and the gaining of confidence and self-respect.

Learned early on,
the benefits of self-discipline
will stay with you throughout your lifetime,
helping you to navigate your world
and realize your goals and dreams.

Aren't you so excited?

We know that parents who empathize with
their children's feelings – rather than coerce,
manipulate, or scare them into obedience –
build stronger, kinder, more resilient kids
with fewer psychological problems.

~ Linda and Ty Hatfield & Wendy Thomas Russell,
ParentShift

Discipline

Discipline is important, and the style we choose will have a lasting impact on our children.

Researchers have found that the old "authoritarian" style of parenting, which involves strict rules, little or no cooperative feedback, and harsh consequences is much less effective than the "authoritative" style of parenting, where parents have high, yet reasonable expectations for behavior. **Authoritative parents set clear rules and consequences, yet encourage warm and responsive ongoing communication with their children.**[9] Positive Discipline calls this approach being kind and firm,[10] and Linda and Ty Hatfield & Wendy Thomas Russell (in their excellent book entitled *ParentShift*), call this "heart-centered" parenting.[11] ~ Lisa Guy

Discipline can benefit the long-term development of a child's mind.

As parents, we have a strong desire to extinguish bad behaviors in our children. And of course! It's hard to tolerate poor behavior at times. When our children "act out," we can look at discipline as not just changing behavior but also something which will benefit the long-term development of their minds as well as build our relationship with them. As Dan Siegel and Tina Bryson explain in *No-Drama Discipline*[12], discipline is an invitation to help our children learn to do things in the right way. When we give them frequent opportunities to "re-do" their misbehaviors, all involved will benefit! Another discipline strategy is to connect first and then redirect when the child is calm. For example, if a child is slapping her mother on the back while she is on the phone, the mother can first connect with her daughter, kneel down at eye level and explain: "I see you're mad." Then redirect: "I won't let you hurt my body. Let's sit here while I talk and you can color until I'm finished." Both the parent and child must be in a calm state for the discipline to be effective. Getting to know the individual temperament of our children and understanding that the brain is wired through repetition and practice can help to minimize disciplinary challenges. In addition, working through difficulties successfully with our children will help to build resilience and model good interpersonal skills. ~ Lea Payne Scott; Social and Behavioral Health Educator

Parents and caregivers can aspire to be patient and loving teachers as they share the skills of discipline and positive repetition with their children.

Most new parents eagerly look forward to teaching their little ones new skills – using a spoon for the first time, writing their name, or riding a bike. Parents have boundless patience for coaching these "fun" skills, and can't imagine losing their temper or being frustrated as their child learns to crawl down stairs or zip a jacket. We need to give the same patience and positive repetition to the skills of discipline, and be understanding when our children get it wrong many, many times while they are learning. Sharing with siblings, being polite, finding positive outlets for big feelings, treating materials with respect, and following directions are all challenging new skills for children to learn, and as their parents we owe them kindness and patience as they practice. Discipline comes from the Latin root which means "to teach or guide." We can be our children's best and most loving teachers. ~ Denise Indvik; Age 55; 3 Children; Parent Education Instructor

Chapter 3
Reflections

Notes for Chapter 3 – Refer back for quick reminders!

Chapter 4

Raising Connected Children – Purpose and Meaning Come from a Sense of Unity

"With each habit we design, each tiny success we celebrate, and each change we make, we reach beyond our personal lives. We shape our families, communities, and societies through our actions. And they shape us. The behaviors we perpetuate matter. It's about becoming the person you want to be - and creating the kind of family, team, community and world we want to live in."
~ BJ Fogg, PhD, Tiny Habits, The Small Changes That Change Everything[1]

Unity

The happiest times of my life have involved coming together with other people. A feeling of connectedness – shared values and dreams – family, friends, neighbors, co-workers, and community members working together toward a common goal. I love people of all kinds, all ages, ethnicities, socio-economic backgrounds, and educational levels. It saddens and confuses me to see so many separate groups resistant to intermingling – unwilling and unable to find common ground.

In the 5th grade, at Malcom X Elementary School in Berkeley, California, my teacher gathered the class into a circle and had us join hands. She turned on "Love Train" by the O'Jay's and my heart soared – "Yes! I thought…this is how it should be." When the O'Jay's sang, "People all over the world, join hands, start a love train, love train," tears came to my eyes and I looked around the circle at my classmates, feeling such a sense of joy and connectedness. Throughout my life, I have longed for unity.

We all come into this world with certain gifts -- we are responsible for sharing them. As parents, we bring very different qualities to our relationship and our children benefit as long as we are unified in our approach to parenting. It is up to us to help identify and nurture our children's gifts and aptitudes, while modeling kindness, compassion, and respect for the gifts of others.

When a child is born, the family unit is of the utmost importance, beginning with the parents, and then branching out to extended family. Parents are a child's first and most important teachers, and often children will learn from what they see their parents do, more readily than from what they hear them say. The nuclear family may look different now than in past years, but it remains essential to build lasting adult relationships to surround and support our children. Parents must nurture their relationship with each other as well, giving time, attention, and care to their partner along with their child.

As we grow to recognize the beautiful connection all living beings share, we must find a way to love and understand one another, while taking responsibility for the health of our planet and natural surroundings. ~ Lisa Guy

Love Section 1

Oh, my precious one
you fill my heart with such love.

A deep affection
that grows with time –
love can take many forms
and invoke a myriad of feelings.

Love between a parent and a child,
a mother and a father,
ourselves and other beings
and the earth that we are blessed to live upon,
can bring tremendous joy
as well as a host of other strong emotions.

I love you unconditionally,
and will do my best to demonstrate that love
through my words and actions,
so we may build a strong foundation of trust
and you can grow and flourish.

Can you feel my love?

You feed babies on one end, wipe them on the other, and love them in between.
~ Dr. Lou Tedone, Pediatrician, Father of 9

Love

Love brings deep meaning to our lives and can change everything for the better. As parents, our own mental and emotional health greatly impacts our lives and those of our children! When we're able to love ourselves unconditionally, secure in our own worth and value, we can then expand our love outward to the world at large. Loving ourselves and our children unconditionally is the key. Children need the love of their parents in order to grow and thrive.
~ Lisa Guy

Children sense and respond to love from their earliest days.

When I was born, I had two older sisters, ages 10 and 13. My mother loved her daughters, but both she and my father were hoping their next child would be a son. Instead, they had me, and strangely, at three months of age I stopped being interested in eating and was failing to thrive. My mother took me to the doctor, and said, "I don't know what the problem is. I feed it, I clean it, I take care of it. . ." and the doctor replied, "Yes, but do you love her?"

While my mother was carrying me, she had clearly imagined her little boy. When I was born, she was devastated. She fell into a depression and resented me. I had taken the place of her long-desired son – she felt as if he had been taken from her. As an infant, on some level I recognized this and consequently was not doing well.

As my mother has told me, upon hearing those words from the doctor, she broke down in tears, allowing all of the pent-up emotions to come forward, and began looking at her baby girl in a whole new light. Amazingly, I sensed this change, felt her love, and resumed eating once again. My mother and I have been close ever since.

There are many reasons for a young child to fail to thrive and I am so grateful to my mother's doctor for recognizing the situation. He helped my mother to understand and address her emotions, which allowed her love for me to come through, loud and clear.
~ Renoda Campbell; Age 58; 2 Children; Professional Photographer/College Academic Advisor

"Every child has a unique way of feeling loved. When you discover your child's love language - and how to speak it - you can build a solid foundation for your child to trust you and flourish as they grow." ~ Gary Chapman and Ross Campbell, The 5 Love Languages of Children[2]

Note: The 5 Love Languages include: (1) Physical Touch; (2) Words of Affirmation; (3) Quality Time; (4) Gifts; and (5) Acts of Service.

Family Section 2

Little one, welcome to our family ~ we're so happy you are here!
As you grow our family will become stronger.

We can benefit from the insight, encouragement and support of our elders,
as well as work toward building a network of friends and community.

You can count on us to be here for you through thick and thin,
providing guidance and boundaries for your safety,
love, and valuable life lessons.

We will catch you when you fall,
find you when you're lost,
and surround you with optimism and hope.

Times may not always be easy
but you can be sure, come what may
we will be here for each other.

Isn't this good to know?

"When our children were young, my husband and I began the tradition of holding weekly family meetings, making them a priority. Over the years, we found these gatherings to be the key to strengthening our family bonds, as we took the weekly opportunity to connect, discuss upcoming events, and teach social and life skills, morals and values. Each of our six children had a chance to lead the meetings, starting as early as age 3, with our help."
~ Deanne Ririe, Parent Educator, Mother of 6

Family

Bringing children into our lives will change things forever.

Several years ago I worked with a young coach who had two little ones. His life had changed significantly with the birth of his children, and he was doing the best to juggle the responsibilities of work, marriage and being a father. One day he asked me, "When will I have my life back again?" How could I help him to understand that this *is* his life, and he and his family will thrive if he can expand his outlook and his new role to family-size? Children add another layer of complexity to our lives, yet there is no doubt they make our life experience infinitely more rewarding! ~ Anonymous Father/
Grandfather; Age 65, Baseball Coach

Research has identified five protective factors[3] that work together to ensure the healthy development of children.

Parents and Caregivers, do you have the following:
(1) Parental Resilience - the ability to manage stress and cope with all types of challenges?

(2) Social Connections - Friends, family, neighbors, and community members who provide emotional support and a sense of belonging?

(3) An understanding of child development - knowledge of ages, stages and expectations for behavior and needs?

(4) Concrete Support - a place to turn to for help when life hits a bump in the road?

(5) An understanding of the social and emotional development of children - to help interact positively with others and communicate emotions effectively?

"Sending kids to look for belonging outside their families carries many risks. Emotionally hungry kids are more likely to fall into unhealthy relationships, engage in high-risk behavior and to experience addiction. That's partially because their relationships with primary caregivers are disconnected, which causes children great stress." ~ Linda & Ty Hatfield & Wendy Thomas Russell, ParentShift[5]

In times of crisis, friends, teachers, and community can lift up families and see them through.

Family has always been important to me. Almost two years ago my wife passed from cancer – our three young children and I were devastated. This strong, kind and wonderful mother and wife had just slowly faded away. . . and when she was gone, I found myself numb and nearly incapacitated. All the things she'd done for our family with such ease for years, were now my sole responsibility, and I didn't know how I was going to carry on. But deep down, I knew I didn't have a choice – regardless of how I was feeling, our kids needed me. Thankfully, our community stepped in and surrounded our family with care and support. An outpouring of food, kindness and love helped to lift us all up and move us forward with our lives. ~ Anthony; Age 57; 3 Children

Community Section 3

We are social beings,
and our human nature can connect us deeply to one another.
We're often happiest when we feel a part
of a supportive group of friends or community.

Bringing our gifts together for the good of the whole is a beautiful thing.
As you grow you will realize your own gifts
and learn how best to share them with those around you.

We gain strength from giving and receiving love and assistance.
Having strong, multigenerational support
and reciprocal relationships we can rely on
is so important for us and for our family.

Won't it be fun to build our community?

"As a long-time elementary and middle school teacher, I
have counseled many parents about the benefits of helping
our children choose their friends wisely when very young,
and then using discussions to gently guide them to make
positive friend and group choices as they grow and mature."
~ Lynn Stafford, Mother of 3

Community

I have been helping my daughter to build her 'community' since she was little by volunteering at school, getting to know her classmates and their families, and organizing playdates and gatherings. Most recently, I have hosted a 'Lunch Bunch' group at our house. Five girls gather weekly during lunch and I provide them with something tasty to eat. One of the other girls has a grandmother who does the same, and opens her home while they each bring a sack lunch and she provides drinks. We can help our children foster positive friendships and build a supportive community. ~ Justine Heinsen, Mother of 2

New parents and caregivers can work to build their community early on.

My best advice for new moms is to build your community. Find the people who lift you up as a mom and can relate to what you're going through. To help find a group of people you "click" with, consider joining a newborn parent group or class - this can enhance the well-being of the entire family! Playdates, outings with the kids, "mom's night out," and babysitting swaps are loads of fun and can enrich the early parenting years. Building community models good social behavior to our children and provides built-in "cousins" and "forever friendships." We had "family" dinners where no one was actually family, as well as vacations and summer camps together. These "cousins" still remain some of my very best friends. We all value this gift of community as we continue the tradition with our own little ones. ~ Brittany Selvy; Age 33; 2 Children; Transitional Kindergarten Teacher

We can teach our children to be sensitive to the needs of others in their community.

My parents taught my brother, sister, and me good morals and values, gave us a solid work ethic, and instilled in us a strong moral consciousness. The message was always, "We were put on this earth to help others!" My grandmother lived near the train station in town and would always keep a pot of soup on the stove to feed the hungry in search of work. My father, mother and two uncles were all activists, fighting causes always related to the fair treatment of fellow humans.

It stands to reason that I felt compelled to do something for the growing homeless population in my community. In 2013, we founded "Hope's Village of SLO," a local nonprofit tasked with the challenge of building a sustainable community village of tiny houses for unhoused veterans and their families. Hope's Village is dedicated to establishing a safe, healthy, and drug-free village community – a place where veterans and others without homes (and with little or no income), can live in dignity and peace. ~ Becky Jorgeson; Age 70; 2 Children; Founder of Hope's Village of SLO

Kindness Section 4

"Kindness is like snow.
It beautifies everything it covers."
~Kahlil Gibran

I will do my best to embody kindness
in our interactions
so you may experience the value
in being kind.

Compassion, empathy, honesty, love,
and a commitment to helping others
will serve you well throughout your life,
and help to make our community and the greater world
a better place.

*Let's remind each other to be compassionate and kind,
okay?*

"It's important to
be kind, rather
than right."

~ Wayne Dyer, Self-Help
Author, Motivational
Speaker

Kindness

"I've come to see that nice and kind are worlds apart. Nice doesn't ask that much of us. It's doing the safe thing, the polite thing, taking the easy and expected action . . . I see kindness as a verb - one that can be summed up by the phrase, 'extend yourself.'" ~ Donna Cameron, Author, Speaker

☆   ☆   ☆

Teaching our children the value of giving has many benefits for our world.

"Granny Annette," my immigrant grandmother from Russia, has always been a positive force in my life. She provided me with an infinite amount of love and support and taught me the value of giving. On a very limited income, Granny saved coins to give to others. She invited her friends over for lunch and passed a jar around to collect money for UNICEF. Every Halloween she gave me a UNICEF can to collect coins from neighbors for those in need. Only then could I accept candy. I have followed my grandmother's example with my own children, grandchildren, and most recently, my great-grandchildren. I want them to experience the power of giving as well. ~ Leslie Rotstein; Age 80; 3 Children; 7 Grandchildren; 3 Great grandchildren; Former Teacher/Current Business Owner and Director of Womenade Non-Profit, Los Osos Cares

☆   ☆   ☆

Developing a habit of treating all those with whom we interact with kindness, can create ripples of positivity.

Kindness represents a deep respect and reverence for all living things. Every action a person takes, however small, begins a series of events. Kindness ensures those events will be positive. Our children look to us to make sense of the world, and we must make a conscious effort, always, to model kindness. Years ago, an experience I had with my teenage son and his friends taught me a valuable lesson. Although we may not realize it, our words, actions, and attitude as we relate to others can have a lasting impact. I served as a chaperon for a team of 10 boys at a 24-hour high school relay event, and needless to say, I was exhausted toward the end. I did my best to interact with the boys, encouraging and connecting with each of them. Several weeks later I attended a meeting with the relay participants and their parents. At the end of the meeting a woman approached to tell me that I had made a tremendous impact on her son. I had no idea who her son was, his name, or even what he looked like. This lesson affected me greatly, as I discovered the words and actions we choose can profoundly impact, encourage, or uplift others, even if we are completely unaware of it. Developing the habit of treating all those with whom we interact, with kindness can create ripples of positivity, which may reach the far corners of our world. ~ Tracy Owen, Age 64; 2 Children; 3 Grandchildren; Past Vocational Rehabilitation Counselor/ Therapeutic Riding Instructor/Equine Therapist/Community Volunteer

Respect Section 5

Dear child,
we all deserve to be treated with dignity,
and we will endeavor always to use a respectful tone
when speaking to you.
We will ask you to afford us, as well as others,
the same courtesy throughout your life.

As you grow,
we will do our best to encourage your curiosity
and provide you with direct, honest responses
as you make your way through life.

Providing you with boundaries
will help to make you feel secure,
and staying calm, unruffled, and in control
will allow us to establish
a solid foundation of trust and respect.

Can we always remember to respect one another?

"People will forget
what you said, people
will forget what you
did, but people will
never forget how you
made them feel."
~ Maya Angelou,
Poet, Activist

Respect

Our children benefit when we explain things clearly in a gentle voice.

After much research on how to be the very best parent possible, one of the things that stands out most clearly in my mind is a child's desire to be treated with respect. Even before my daughter could speak, I explained things clearly to her in a gentle voice: "Let's change your diaper . . . it's no fun to be wet!", or "Let's put on your jacket now, it's cold outside. . ." During this time, I realized I would not be happy if someone quickly laid me on a table, and pulled down my pants to change my diaper. . . or grasped my arm and put it into the sleeve of a coat! Engaging with our children in a calm, respectful way teaches them how to interact with others. ~ Victoria Andrews; Age 30; 1 Child; Retail Sales

Both parents/caregivers and children need mutual respect.

The last time my son Santiago and I had a disagreement was two years ago, when he was six. I don't remember what the issue was, but I do remember what he said: "I don't love you anymore." "That's okay," I replied. I went on to tell him that I loved him enough for both of us, and if he decided to love me back a little, that would be great – but what I really needed from him was his respect. Our children need us to be the adult, first and foremost. I pride myself in working hard, and prioritize my family - it's important for my children to develop these same values. Santiago has a PlayStation, but in order for him to spend time playing with it, he first has to complete his daily chores around the house. I make a point of treating him with respect, giving him increased responsibilities as he grows older, and expecting him to show me respect in return. I learned this from my father, and he from his. Our children look to us to learn how to behave and conduct their lives. What we say is important, but it's what we do that really matters. ~ Ranferi "Jose," Age 40; 1 Child; Contractor

We can encourage our children to stand up for themselves and others.

My 14-year-old son had a disturbing encounter with another student while riding the bus to school one morning. He's not sure what prompted it, but the other student yelled out loudly to him, "Why don't you just go back to Mexico?" As he relayed the story to me, I was happy about two things. The first was that several of his friends and fellow band members were there and told the bully to back off and stop bothering him – when people stick together and stand up for those being treated badly, the power of a bully is taken away. The second was that he felt comfortable enough to talk to me about it. I told him that a bully can only hurt you if you allow him to. I also said he has every right to be living on the Central Coast, and to be treated with respect. This experience gave us a chance to talk about the fact that he can be proud of our family and where we've come from, and how important it is to stand up for ourselves and others. ~ Luis; Age 32; 3 Children; Landscape Design and Maintenance

Forgiveness Section 6

None of us are perfect
and at one time or another in our lives,
we all will make mistakes.

Let's learn to forgive ourselves and others,
as transforming feelings of hurt and anger will help us to heal
and live in harmony among our family and community.

Once we have forgiven someone,
we must decide to renew or release the relationship.
If we decide to renew, we may build a new relationship –
if we decide to release, we are free to move on.

FORGIVENESS,
By Adelaide Vanden Bossche, Age 25

Forgiveness flutters around us
Not always easy to find or capture. . .
The mystical inconsistency
Sometimes swiftly plucked from the sky
Other times sought for an eternity.

It is a grace that requires effort and awareness;
Whether it be personal or interpersonal. . .
One cannot demand forgiveness ~ it must be given freely.

An unaccepting mindset must first be conquered.
Acceptance, a companion to ride with
On one's quest for forgiveness ~
Without it we can get lost within anger
Frozen in a bleak world of resentment
Unable to unlock possibilities and inner potential
Harming ourselves and those we care for in the process.

Allow yourself permission to forgive
A chance to grasp the elusive creature
And the recognition that you are better off
Once it is held gently within your heart.

Forgiveness

Learning to forgive ourselves and others is a gift for us, as well as our families.

Our youngest child was diagnosed with a brain stem tumor when he was just 3 months old. I spent almost a year at Stanford Medical Center with him as he went through treatment, leaving our three other young children at home with my husband. The cancer little Jack had was extremely rare, and from the beginning I somehow felt it was my fault he was sick.

The roller coaster of emotions was devastating, as he was diagnosed, went through surgery, treatment, and was said to be in remission; it returned, and in a location on his brain said to be inoperable. I hung on for dear life and barely maintained that grip when he finally departed. That first year after Jack died, it was all I could do to get the kids off to school before crawling back into bed and allowing the exhaustion to take over. People would ask, "How are your other kids doing?" and I honestly didn't know. I knew I was failing them but was powerless to pull myself out of the deep hole I found myself in. I simply didn't have the capacity to engage with them, or anyone else for that matter.

With the help of a therapist, as the months passed I began to find the strength to get out of bed, and read books about healing from loss. I spoke honestly to my children about the hard time I was having. Wherever life may lead us, I believe we always have another chance. What matters most is that we do our best to give our kids the love and emotional support they need. I finally learned how to forgive myself – for taking the blame when Jack became ill . . .for failing my other children by not being physically, mentally or emotionally there during Jack's illness and the year after he passed.

While our family experienced unthinkable trauma and sadness, by embracing the love we shared, communicating, and striving to build happiness back into our lives, we have continued on. Best of all, we treasure our family as the precious gift that it is and has always been. ~ Bridget Ready; Age 62; 4 Children; Retired Elementary Teacher/ Founder of Jack's Helping Hand – local nonprofit for children with cancer and medically fragile special need

★   ★   ★

"Forgiveness – whether we need it or bestow it – is a miraculous gift." ~ Unknown

Changing Fate Section 7

Oh, dear one –
if we as parents have experienced difficult circumstances early in life,
or have made less than ideal choices as we entered adolescence or adulthood,
we may believe our options in life are limited and our fate has been set.

But we can make a conscious choice to work towards healing ~
one that protects us and enables us to grow and thrive.
We can exert our free will. . . imagine the life we'd like to live,
and do what we can to make it a reality.

First, we can take steps towards self-compassion and self-understanding,
and then make sense of our history by telling our life story.
We can recount the facts, identify our feelings
and embrace a message of resilience.
Journaling, therapy, talking to friends ~
these are all things which allow us to put words to the feelings
and move forward, toward a place of forgiveness.

We know it will help to align with others
who embody healthy goals and values,
and establish boundaries with those who do not.

Finding our place within a loving, supportive community
can provide the impetus for positive change.

Let's look to the future with hope and determination!

> **We are always in a perpetual state of being created and creating ourselves**
> ~ Dan Siegel, Physician, Author

Changing Fate

Left untreated, trauma can be passed on from one generation to the next.

Too many parents affected by trauma haven't had the opportunity to put a name to the thing (aka trauma) that has plagued them for years. Left untreated, these parents can pass on trauma to their children, and the cycle goes on and on. During my years as a school nurse, I have worked with many children who have experienced trauma. I've learned ways of helping them to calm their emotions which often manifest in physical symptoms such as crying, shaking, and increased heart and respiratory rates. Mindfulness, consistency, and positive relationships are highly effective in helping those who have experienced trauma to heal.
~ Grace Van Doren; Age 49; 3 Children; Lead Credentialed School Nurse

Understanding what lies beneath our triggers can help to parent from a calm place.

I teach parents about the brain and how the nervous system reacts in stressful situations with our children. Things our little ones do may elicit responses from us as parents that are tethered to memories of the past. When these triggers occur, it is an invitation for us to make sense of what happened and why we are experiencing these strong emotions. We can do this by "creating a coherent narrative," or telling the story that contains the facts, feelings and message of resilience, as Dan Siegel and Tina Payne Bryson explain in their book, *The Whole-Brain Child* [4]. Over time, with practice, we can learn to be more mindful – creating a pause between our own impulses and reactions. An example I use in my classes is of a parent who noticed her response each time her daughter screamed loudly or had a meltdown in a restaurant. She realized this behavior repeatedly caused her to freeze with internal panic. Afterwards, when she realized the pattern, she shared her experience with her husband. She eventually came to understand she was being triggered by former experiences she'd had as a child with her own father, when he had exploded unpredictably. Making this connection and understanding that her daughter was behaving in a normal way for a toddler helped this parent regulate her emotions and stay calm and emotionally stable during future incidents. ~ Lea Payne Scott; M.P.H, Social and Behavioral Health Educator

It is possible to consciously and purposefully change our fate.

My husband comes from a family with a long line of trauma. Growing up, he was determined to break the cycle, and thank goodness, he has succeeded. Early on, my husband took notes about what he wanted to do differently, and how he did NOT want to live his life. He has always loved young people and has been a high school P.E. teacher and football coach for the past 20+ years. Not only is he a stellar father to my children from a previous marriage, but he is able to make a huge difference in the lives of a vast array of young students each year – many of whom do not have fathers of their own at home. While it's not possible for us to change our own personal history, we can use our experiences to change our lives in a positive way. ~ Anonymous; Mother of 2

Honoring our Ancestors, Elders, and Family Traditions Section 8

Our family has a long and rich history
including many generations,
stories, and family traditions.

We will teach you about our family's past,
and model how to treat elders with respect –
both within our family and in the greater community.

We'll also do our best to help you understand the cycle of life,
and learn that all things have their time.

Let us value the perspective and life experiences,
as well as the gifts of wisdom of those who came before us.

Not only will our family enjoy traditions
which have been handed down from past generations,
but we will create new traditions of our own.

Doesn't this sound wonderful?

"Knowing your generational
story firms the ground upon
which you stand. It makes
your life, your struggles and
triumphs, bigger than your
lone existence. It connects
you to a grand plotline."

~ Cicely Tyson, Model
and Actress

68

Honoring our Ancestors, Elders, and Family Traditions

"There is much talk of progress . . . moving forward into the future with high tech and robots. Efficient but heartless. So much interest in what's out there, while I yearn for what's in here - remnants of what once was. Planting seeds in fertile ground. . . wearing clothes spun and woven by living hands. . . hands making tools out of steel and fire. Our ancestors lived grounded and passed it on for us to stand on. Let's give them some thought, and some thanks. . . for you see, something solid to stand on is food for your soul." ~ Mary Pellegrino, Mother of 1, Grandmother of 5

Feeling a connection with our ancestors can provide a sense of stability and grounding.

My mother had a quiet way about her. It was her connection to her ancestors, passed on to me, that has allowed me to feel a continuation of life which provides a sense of stability and grounding. It was partly through the love and care she gave keepsakes such as her grandmother's crystal vase, or in the way she made the Thanksgiving feast and prepared the beautiful table with her mother's china, silver polished and linens pressed, that shared the energy of reverence and connection. Yet always, it wasn't about the things so much as the love they represented. Her embodiment of that love was the true gift she shared with her family, as it served also to honor those who came before her.

Again, it was by example that my mother helped us know how to be in the company of elders. She always called adults by their surname with the appropriate title. There were two older couples that were given the honorary title of Uncle and Aunt who had a special role in our young lives. Uncle Ralph and Aunt Lois were very casual, what we might call "kid friendly." And yet, I remember equally fondly our Aunt Billie and Uncle Harry. Aunt Billie had this amazingly perfect home with treasures everywhere. We knew that inside we were not to touch, run around or be loud. In fact, inside meant mostly being in a chair. Outside we could play and be wild, even asking Uncle Harry to take out his false teeth for us to see! Understanding the rules of a place and the importance of that information was an additional bonus learned from these loving elders.

My own two children are grown now, and together we deepen established traditions through intention, while allowing creativity to guide in the evolution of "new" family traditions. I am amazed how a simple round of gratitude at the beginning of a meal brings our voices together in unity as we celebrate the bounty of this earth and the beauty of remembering what we each are grateful for in that moment. ~ Marie McRee; Age 62; 2 Children; Mentor/Anchor/Community Service

"We must remind our children that the love, influence, traditions, and memories of our loved ones will carry on for generations to come." ~ Jill Garman, Bereavement Counselor

Beauty of Nature Section 9

Oh, my love,
every living thing on earth is intrinsically connected.

As you grow, we will help to cultivate
your awareness and appreciation of nature
and the universal responsibility we all share to protect our planet.

Picnics on the grass, walks in the hills,
riding bikes, and playing at the beach and park –
we can plant vegetables and flowers in the garden,
watch the moon and stars at night, and listen to the owls' hoot. . .

Let's enjoy, contemplate, and delight in our natural surroundings.

Come. . . shall we go outside?

Joy comes from simple and natural things – mists over meadows, sunlight on leaves, the path of the moon over water. Even rain and wind and stormy clouds bring joy, just as knowing animals and flowers and where they live.

~ Sigurd F. Olson, Author, Environmentalist

Beauty of Nature

Spending time in nature is one of life's greatest gifts.

Don't we all want there to be some beautiful presence walking by our side throughout our life? Maybe there is one. . .My partner and I sat in the park. All around us people were busy getting somewhere else. We sat. Watched a Black Phoebe fly up to a branch. She flicked her tail, flew quick in a swoop, and with the audible snap of her little beak, caught an insect midair before returning to that branch to eat. Her thrill, her happiness, made my partner and me laugh out loud with joy.

Sun filtered down through scattered winter clouds and caught the ever-green leaves of a coast-Live Oak tree. Blue sky stretched our eyes wide. The beauty was free, and right by our sides. Suddenly the birds tensed. The Black Phoebe darted into the safety of a shadow. Up the hill, we could see a flock of birds fleeing for their lives. All around, different birds started sounding calls of fear and alarm. Swooping low amongst houses up the hill, a Cooper's Hawk was on the hunt with lighting-like speed. It could swing into the park in the time it took a Black Phoebe to catch a fly. No bird was safe. In nature, nothing ever forgets that this short precious life hangs by a thread. And the result is a full-blooded flush of exuberant Presence that's always awake, to catch the beauty of each moment passing by, as it makes up the tapestry out of which it all comes, and to which it all goes. The tapestry that's always here. Always there. Present, right by our side. ~ Sam McRee; Age 32; Teacher/Naturalist/Author

We can instill the love of nature in our children.

Nature is my "go to" when I need a change of scenery. Back in my childhood, running outside in the wind, I felt it blow my troubles away. Plopping down on the shore, I let waves envelop me, dry clothes and all. Country roads and tall mountains filled with trees and cows! They all made me happy. So as a parent, I tried to instill in our children the love of nature and being outside. Long walks with newborns can do a world of good for both mother and child. When toddlers are feeling frustrated, the suggestion of "want to go outside?" can be a game changer for their mood – and yours, too! ~ Lisa Katherman; Age 61; 2 Children; 1 grandchild; Mental Health Advocate/Volunteer

Chapter 4
Reflections

Notes for Chapter 4 – Refer back for quick reminders!

Chapter 5

Life Perspective – The Way We Parent and View the World Will Have a Lasting Impact on Our Developing Child

Being knowledgeable about the developmental stage of your child is like giving yourself a big present. Nothing is more soothing to a new parent than knowing that your child's behavior is typical for their age--even though it may be challenging. By understanding ages and stages, you can anticipate and plan for common behavior like sleep regressions, tantrums, separation anxiety, or endlessly throwing food off the highchair! The gift for your child is having a parent who has developmentally appropriate expectations, and doesn't expect too much or too little of them. Find a reputable source for child development information (such as the CDC Milestones checklist[1], or the AAP Healthy Children website[2]) and keep reading it until your kids move out of the house! ~ Denise Indvik, 3 Children, Age 55, Parent Education Instructor

Doing our best to convey a gracious and soft approach in our everyday lives as we parent our children and engage with others can work miracles!

Consider the following poem and whether you'd like to make an effort to embrace these ideas in your own life. Remember that none of us are perfect, and each day brings with it a new opportunity to work toward being the parent we'd like to be.

Gracious and Soft
In My Approach

I'd like to soften my hard edges,
take the stress out of my voice,
sing, and play, and laugh some more,
making this my choice.

I'd like to wake up smiling,
let go of all I can't control,
experience this precious life,
allow things to unfold.

I'd like to focus on the positive,
let faith and hope survive,
I'll listen to opinions,
not always needing to be right.

I'd like to become more accepting,
of tastes and preferences unlike my own,
of funny traits and mannerisms,
of those who are (and aren't yet) grown.

I'd like to try to stop correcting,
determine if a blunder needs mentioning at all,
expect less and inquire more,
lift others when they fall.

I'd like to nurture inner gifts,
of mine and those around,
looking carefully for treasures,
celebrating once they're found.

I'd like to step aside,
allow others to have their say,
asking, "How do you think it should be done?"
rather than forcing the way.

I'd like to greet my family with a loving smile,
no matter what's been done,
forgiving past transgressions,
understanding we are one.

I'd like to learn to really listen,
expand my thinking and perspective,
hear, see, feel, and love more,
learn to be reflective.

These intentions are all worthy,
and I know there are quite a few,
but I'll do my best to honor them,
hoping others in our world will too. . .

~ Lisa and William Guy (Inspired by piece
shared by Stacy Ballantyne)

The Power of Listening <small>Section 1</small>

Little one, we will work on learning to truly listen
to you and others,
as listening is the golden key
that opens the door to healthy human relationships.

Through the years
let's give special attention to creating opportunities to talk
and listen to each other.
If we must postpone our conversation
for one reason or another,
we'll make sure to continue it at another time.

Never fear, my dear
your voice will be heard.

Can you hear me?

"When your child feels loved, when her emotional
tank is full, she will be more responsive to parental
guidance in all areas of her life. She will listen
without resentment." ~ Gary Chapman & Ross Campbell,
The 5 Love Languages[3]

The Power of Listening

Confidence comes from being listened to and heard.

When my first of three sons was born, I learned that sign language was a helpful way of communicating before infants learn to verbalize their needs. It was supposed to be especially helpful during the notorious "terrible twos," and I thought it sounded great to minimize that struggle. I started signing with Tristian when he was around 8 or 9 months old, with some basic, frequently used signs: "milk, all done, water, drink, eat, sleep, potty" and what proved to be the most used, "more." Babies don't sign back to you right away - you must consistently sign every time you say a certain word that you are trying to teach them. I also had baby sign language DVDs I'd pop in now and then.

Eventually each of my three children learned to sign at a year or so. Their signs were never exactly the same as what I had shown them, but I came to learn each of their specific hand motions and was able to respond to them accordingly. Being able to communicate with our babies and truly decipher what they are thinking or what they need at that moment has greatly strengthened our bond with them. Confidence comes from being listened to and heard – it helps our children feel important and valued.

I found the "twos" to be not so terrible, and without many tantrums. By the threes, my boys were all able to verbalize more and the signing slowly faded, but the time that we had that special form of communication was so good. I of course continued the practice with my second and third children. It was fun to get the older child(ren) involved in signing with their siblings, and this helped them form strong bonds together as well. I believe that if we listen to our kids when they're younger, they'll listen to us when they're older! ~ Margaux O'Quest; Age 45; 3 Children; Educator, Community Volunteer

Beginning when our son and daughter were in kindergarten and lasting through high school, my husband and I made a regular practice of picking the kids up from school whenever possible and heading straight to the park or beach. It was a time we all looked forward to, where the kids could decompress after the long school day, collect shells, run in the surf with our family dog, play jump rope with seaweed, and share the fun, interesting and difficult things which had occurred throughout their day. Spending that time together in nature was priceless, and the opportunity to connect and listen to our children every day has helped to cement our tight-knit family. ~ KeAloha Hendey-McKee, Mother of 2

Playtime Section 2

Oh my,
you have so much fun ahead of you!

We will begin by singing, talking, smiling,
and familiarizing you with faces,
learning object permanence as we come and go from view.

We will play with you often and joyfully,
allowing you to touch, smell, taste, hear, and see things.
Playful learning can start with your very first smile,
and early games like "peekaboo" and "where's the baby"
will start us on our way to many years of playtime fun!

We'll do things together
and then I'll encourage you to do them on your own.
Through play, your creativity and critical thinking will be cultivated
and you'll learn how best to communicate with others
and interact with the world around you.

Exploring challenges together
will stretch your abilities and allow you to grow
within the safety of my care.

Won't we have a ball?

"A child's
brain develops when
she experiences a small
amount of positive stress,
and it is the role of the
parent to buffer the stress through
reassurance and stability, helping to bring the
child back to a state of equilibrium."
~ Nisha Abdul Cader, Pediatrician, Mother of 4

Playtime

 Play is a child's work.

Our son Aldin, now five years old, has been attending a Montessori school for the past three years and we have become accustomed to the idea that play is a child's work. Through play, young children learn how to think creatively and use their senses to develop cognitive processing, while growing physically, socially, and emotionally. We also have a two-year-old daughter named Hannah, and it has been a beautiful thing to see the relationship she and her brother have formed. We have watched Hannah teach Aldin how to sit at a table and drink tea from imaginary cups. . . and then we have watched Aldin teach Hannah how to play "Rocket Ships" and also "Zoo," where each plastic animal is sorted, discussed, and placed in its appropriate habitat.

Hannah's physical development is greatly accelerated by playing with her older brother. One night during a "sleepover," which consisted of Aldin sleeping on the floor beside his sister's crib, he climbed inside and showed Hannah how to climb out of her crib, which she happily did and proceeded to come into our bedroom to proudly share her newfound skill! My husband and I let the kids work out their differences on their own as much as possible, and we see them developing their problem-solving abilities, cooperation, and creativity daily. Outside play is especially beneficial, and it's a wonder how much fun the two of them can have with just an old water bottle and an empty egg carton.

We inherited 10 chickens recently and the kids have endless fun with them! Not only do they collect eggs, feed, and care for the chickens, but they ask to rake out their coop, and enjoy pushing them in the stroller and including them in their games. They also take great pride in caring for the chickens, and we've noticed their self-confidence growing with this new responsibility. Our attitude toward "messes" has been evolving, as we recognize the need for (and effectiveness of) planning out activity spaces and anticipating ways to mitigate cleaning issues. Painting most often happens out on the grass, the "water table" has a rule of no dirt anywhere nearby, and my husband is building a new "mud pit" with the use of 4x4's, far away from the sidewalk. ~ Amanda Ferrell; Age 35; 2 Children; Middle School Math Teacher

 Parents who play with their children as well as their peers can model positive behavior.

My dad has always had a passion for basketball – playing, coaching, and watching – which he has shared with my brother and me. As a little girl, he would take me along to the park when he had a game, set me up with a hoop attached to his car, and I would practice my shot while he and his teammates were practicing theirs! His involvement, enthusiasm, and guidance have made such a positive impact on my life. ~ Ashlee Stewart, P.E. Teacher, Age 33

Learning to Share Section 3

As you grow
we will help you to learn the art of sharing.

At first, you'll believe you are the center of the world
and everything belongs to you,
but with guidance and positive role modeling
you will find you are in tune with others,
understanding their point of view as important
and separate from your own.
This is essential to making and keeping friends.

Can we work together to learn to share our love and possessions?

" Love only grows by sharing. You can only have
more for yourself by giving it away to others. "
~ Brian Tracy, Author, Motivational Speaker

Learning to Share

Parents can help lay the groundwork for sharing.

Expecting children under age 3 to freely share toys and materials is setting everyone up for frustration! Toddlers are still developing their sense of empathy, which is foundational to sharing with others. Instead, try playing games of "taking turns" with your little one. When they hand you a toy during play, respond excitedly with "Oh, it's my turn now, thank you!" before handing the toy back and saying "Now it's your turn again!". This type of play can help little ones develop the habit and trust that even if they give something up, it will come back to them eventually. It lays the groundwork for true sharing once the child is developmentally ready, sometime in their third year. ~ Denise Indvik; Age 55; 3 Children; Parent Education Instructor

As parents, we have the unique opportunity to help guide our children as they grow to adulthood.

Our 10-year-old son confided in me recently that when he goes to his friend's house, not a lot of sharing happens. The boys like to play video games, and on the rare occasions when his friend allows him to have a turn, he ends up leaving the room to do something else. My son told me he wished his friend would be nice, like his older brother's best friend, and this confession opened the door to my guidance – I suggested he talk to his friend and let him know how he was feeling. Learning to advocate for ourselves, while communicating areas of concern and approaching interpersonal challenges in a proactive way, are all valuable skills for kids and adults alike!

Shortly thereafter, our 10-year-old received a sleepover invitation from this friend, along with one other boy. He wasn't sure he wanted to go. I suggested he attend the sleepover and take the opportunity to talk to his friend, and that's just what he did. At the beginning of the sleepover, he pulled him aside and explained that he really didn't like it when his friend rarely allowed him to take a turn playing video games, and left the room when he finally did relinquish the controls. He also pointed out other times when he was made to feel uncomfortable and unappreciated. His friend actually heard him, and it turned out to be the best sleepover he'd ever had! I love that as parents, we have the unique opportunity to help guide our children along the path to adulthood. It is not an easy task, but it's full of rewards and joy, as we evolve alongside our developing human beings. ~ Margaux; Age 45, 3 Children; Educator, Community Volunteer

"Happiness comes from helping others, by being with others, and by sharing, even if it's only a smile." ~ Zain Hashmi, Author

79

Recognizing and Encouraging Children's Gifts Section 4

Dear child,
each of us has our own strengths and aptitudes
and it will be wonderful to watch you grow
and see your gifts emerge.

You can be sure we'll be there
to support you as you face your challenges as well!

We will do our best to recognize
and talk with you about your strengths,
providing ample opportunities for you to explore the world
and find your special place within it.

What will your special gifts be?

"We all have different aptitudes, and within a family we can serve one another with our unique abilities. As parents we must be careful not to force children to become replicas of us, or even worse, fulfill the dreams we never accomplished for ourselves."

~ Gary Chapman and Ross Campbell,
The 5 Love Languages of Children

Recognizing and Encouraging Children's Gifts

Viewing our children with curiosity and an open mind can help them grow and succeed.

As a new parent, my perception of our oldest son, Bradley, was a bit distorted. In my eyes, he was easygoing, smart, kind, resourceful, and could do no wrong! Our second son, Dominic, came along just twelve months later, and was hard to handle. Dominic was strong-willed, had multiple temper tantrums, and gave me a great deal of worry. When it was time for our parent/teacher conference for Bradley's kindergarten class, the teacher said he was a normal, well-functioning student, but surprisingly, that was about it. The following year I met with this same kindergarten teacher to discuss Dominic's progress. To my astonishment, the teacher gushed with admiration. . . she couldn't say enough about him - how much he contributed and how well he interacted with her and the other students. Was this the same boy who was so difficult at home? What I have come to learn is that our children often take on different personas depending upon the situation. Coming just one year after Bradley, Dominic likely felt some frustration, and competition, which he did not experience in the classroom, where he could stand alone and bring forth his gifts of caring, contributing, and connecting with others. Having an open mind, really working to see the gifts of our children and having patience and a sense of humor can make all the difference! ~ Anonymous, Age 81; 3 Children; 4 Grandchildren; 7 Great Grandchildren; past Grocery Store Checker and Community Volunteer

Nurturing strengths in our children from an early age will help to build confidence.

A student of mine started out the school year by telling me she had dyslexia. Her confidence was low, and she was hesitant to read aloud in class. We worked together on her reading, and I continued to give her the time and encouragement she needed to develop her confidence. It wasn't long before she was volunteering to read aloud to the class, and as she excelled in her school subjects, I saw a newfound confidence permeate other areas of her life, including her personal relationships. I was able to help her break through the negative perception of herself and see the world (and her place within it) in a different light.

~ Guy Crabb; Age 65; 3 Children; Navy Veteran/Teacher/Historian/Writer/Innovator

Gentle guidance can help our children pursue activities which bring them joy.

Our daughter Grace played the flute in elementary school band, but she lost interest before entering junior high school. Knowing her love for music and believing that she would enjoy the elevated experience of playing in junior high, I strongly encouraged her to continue with band just a little bit longer. My hunch paid off, and I was so happy at the end of her 7th grade year when she told me, 'No matter what kind of day I'm having, when I walk in the door to the band room, I'm happy!' ~ Barbara Martinez, Mother of 2

Faith, Hope and Wonder Section 5

Little one, let's approach life with openness and curiosity,
and do our best to maintain a sense of faith, hope and wonder.
This can help us to experience a feeling of interconnectedness,
see we are a part of something greater than ourselves,
and understand the beauty and value of life.

Take my hand, dear one ~ the world is filled with wonder . . .

"Faith is the centerpiece of a connected life. It allows us to live by the grace of invisible strands. It is a belief in a wisdom superior to our own. Faith becomes a teacher in the absence of fact."
~ Terry Tempest Williams, Writer, Activist

Faith, Hope and Wonder

"If you take in the ordinary wonders of life, they [your children] will feel the depth of your pleasure and learn to experience joy. If you walk with them in the darkness of life's mysteries you will open the gate to understanding. They will learn to see in the darkness and not be afraid." ~ William Martin, The Parent's Tao Te Ching[4]

✩   ✩   ✩

We can all aspire to grow both internally and externally throughout our lives.

As parents, we teach our children through each interaction and shared experience. When our son was young, I developed the ritual of holding him close – breastbone to breastbone – and telling him, "I am filling you with love, courage, and kindness. . . giving you everything you might need to be in the world. . ." As we continued this practice, the more I began to experience these qualities in myself, the more a sense of peace and calm seemed to emanate from within. Along with this came a desire to share with others the love and peace I felt, as I worked with new parents and encouraged them to connect with what they wished their parents had given them in their early years.

I believe we all should aspire to grow both internally and externally throughout our lives. Internal growth has to do with how we feel inside, where our thinking leads, and what our "gut" tells us. If we're feeling strengthened, encouraged or curious, we're likely on a good path. If we feel ashamed, diminished, or a sense of guilt, we are not on a path which leads to wholeness. The external aspect of our development provides a way to assess how we're advancing in relation to others. Are we learning to be more kind, generous, and patient – not only with our family but with those who might be more challenging? Often, this is where an institution or a prescribed spiritual practice can be helpful, by providing external benchmarks as well as a community of fellow travelers.

Recognizing our sense of connection to something bigger than ourselves, developing a search for meaning and purpose in our lives, and practicing tolerance while allowing others the freedom to believe, even though their paths may be different than our own, are gifts – not only to ourselves, but to our children and our world. ~ Nancy Feniuk Nelson; Age 68; 1 Child; Retired Lutheran Pastor

✩   ✩   ✩

"When we calm our minds and listen deeply, we can begin to experience the synchronicity of life. . .

. . . and notice the signs with wonder, having the awareness that we are all connected – to each other and to every living being." ~ J. Elizabeth Diggle, Executive Coach

Fostering Unconditional Love
Trust and Faith in Baby Section 6

We love you with all our hearts
no matter what,
and trust that you will develop
along your own unique path
in your own way
and according to your very own timeline.

While providing a rich environment for you to explore,
we will leave behind all worries
and have faith in your personal journey.

Do you realize how special you are?

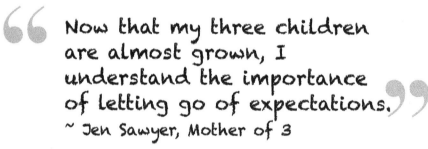

Now that my three children
are almost grown, I
understand the importance
of letting go of expectations.
~ Jen Sawyer, Mother of 3

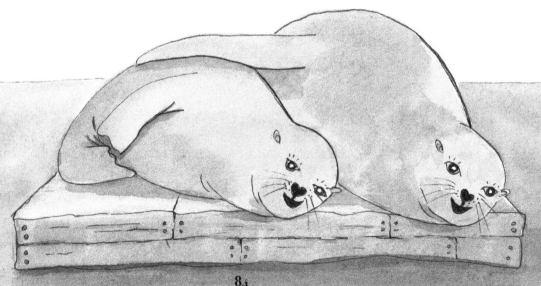

Fostering Unconditional Love Trust and Faith in Baby

"I was so hard on myself early on. . . believing my children had to stick to a rigid schedule, planning outings and being disappointed when they didn't turn out as I had hoped, expecting my babies to be calm and feeling nervous when they weren't. . . so much surrender goes along with parenthood. We cannot completely control how our day goes, what our children will be drawn to, or who they will be. We must love them unconditionally, gently guide and support them as they grow, and celebrate the people they are." ~ Jen Sawyer, Mother of 3

☆　　　☆　　　☆

We can show our children we love them, no matter what.

It wasn't until I became a parent that I began to search out what it means to love a child unconditionally. How does a child experience this? How would a child know deep in his or her soul that my love is unflinching, firmly rooted beyond circumstance and performance? I have found the answer in the little moments. I have honestly, humbly found it in how I respond in the un-glamorous, mundane, and often difficult moments of everyday life as a parent.

My children seem to test me A LOT. Just before sitting down to write this, our overtired baby was screaming at me, and now my toddler is crying and whining at her dad for some reason only understood by two-year-olds. Kids seem to have a way of taking a normal day and turning it upside down. And yet, despite the stressors, I know somewhere in my heart the call is to love anyway. To respond with patience, kindness, and self-control. Even (or especially) when I need to discipline my little ones. Even when my toddler hits the baby for attention, and my mama bear heart growls inside. Even when I'm embarrassed by the very public tantrum. . . I love you, dear children - for who you are, just as you are. And I promise, in the little moments, not to make you feel guilt or shame, as I gently discipline and guide you through a myriad of growth experiences. You are enough. Just as you are, my perfectly imperfect children.
~ Erika Pruett; Age 33; 2 Children; Graphic and Web Designer

☆　　　☆　　　☆

Understanding a child's unique temperament can help him to thrive.

Temperament describes the way we each approach and react to the world, and while it does not directly predict behavior, it can help parents and caregivers to better understand how young children approach and relate to the world around them. Researchers generally categorize children into three temperament types: Easy or flexible, Active or feisty, and Slow to warm or cautious.[5] However, all children's temperaments do not fall neatly into one of the three types, and it's important to note that although a child's temperament does not change over time, the intensity of temperamental traits can be affected by a family's cultural values and parenting styles. Understanding a child's unique temperament can help parents and caregivers to identify strengths and understand the supports needed to succeed in both their relationships and their environment. ~ Nadine McCarty, 64; 2 children; Retired Parent Education Instructor

Failure - a Temporary Defeat Section 7

Mistakes are opportunities to learn.
We learn the most when we are pushing outside our boundaries
and making an effort to grow and try new things.
As parents, we will make mistakes
and as a child, you will make them too.

Somewhere along the way we will likely make bad decisions
or find ourselves in difficult situations.
The important thing is that we recognize our mistakes
and make adjustments in the future.

We'll do our best to support your efforts to learn
and take more of a lighthearted approach toward mistakes,
encouraging you to look for areas of improvement
and continue to work toward mastering goals.
As you practice new things, we'll accept your efforts
and take care not to redo them ourselves.

Do not be afraid when you face an edge or challenge –
we will help you to move ahead, undaunted, without fear of failure.

Remember, learning from our mistakes is the key!

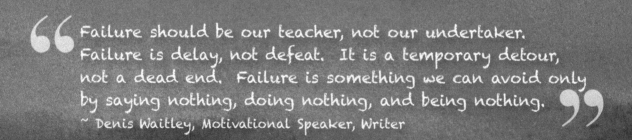

Failure should be our teacher, not our undertaker.
Failure is delay, not defeat. It is a temporary detour,
not a dead end. Failure is something we can avoid only
by saying nothing, doing nothing, and being nothing.
~ Denis Waitley, Motivational Speaker, Writer

Failure—a Temporary Defeat

Questions and uncertainty may arise as we become new parents or caregivers. . . the key is to be determined to learn and grow alongside our little ones. . .

☆   ☆   ☆

Russell Swanagon is overcome with a love like no other as he holds his newborn son awkwardly in his arms and greets him with an apology – "I'm sorry!" He is speaking of the mistakes and blunders he knows he'll make in the future--because he doesn't know how to be a father. He is determined to learn, and as the days and weeks pass, his wife (a pediatric nurse) teaches him how to change diapers, bottle feed, and tend to his son's needs. He learns these things, but deeply wishes to be the best father he can be. . . a father in his own way! Russell is an avid reader. But when he begins sharing with his infant son the words of the novel he is currently reading, "Tropic of Cancer" by Henry Miller (labeled obscene by censors) his wife threatens him with a wooden spoon dripping tomato sauce: "You had better find something more appropriate to read to our son!" So, he begins a search for more child-friendly stories and comes across Winnie the Pooh. We join Russell now in his quest for excellence as a father:

> *"Here is Edward Bear, coming downstairs now, bump, bump, bump, on the back of his head, behind Christopher Robin. It is, as far as he knows, the only way of coming downstairs, but sometimes he feels that there really is another way, if only he could stop bumping for a moment and think of it." Winnie-the-Pooh, by A. A. Milne[6]*

As I read these words, it occurred to me that this is exactly how I felt about my own life: There must be a better way, but I can't stop bumping long enough to think of it. After a bit, I picked the book up again and read it through to the end in one sitting. I was enthralled by the stories, the characters and the wisdom, and I could not wait to share this book with my son. This was the first of countless books and stories that we read together every night until my son was in 8th grade. This bond allowed us to share intimate, quality time together each night and we had valuable, open conversations about the characters and situations in the stories we read, allowing us to develop understanding and empathy for those who are different from ourselves; to think critically about the decisions and situations that characters found themselves in, and to relate the events and archetypes in the story to our own lives. All of this provided a strong foundation upon which to build our relationship.

When our younger son came along, I had learned so much about being a father, and things came much more easily. My oldest son is now a man and himself a father of a fine boy. He is confident, self-assured and supportive, reading to his own son every night, just as we did when he was a child. ~ Russell Swanagon; Age 66; 3 Children; University Professor/Storyteller/Writer

Building Resilience and Courage Section 8

Dear one,
throughout your life, we will help to build your resilience
by showing you can count on us
for open communication, encouragement, and support.

We understand that praising your effort before your intellect
will help to foster your determination.

When challenges arise, we'll do our best
to help you see what can be gained
from these difficult experiences,
and this knowledge will help to promote your resilience
and develop your courage and character.

We all experience some amount of pain, difficulty, and misfortune
during our lifetime,
but the way we perceive and work through these events and circumstances
is the very way we build our strength.
We will help you to learn to help yourself.

Did you know, you have an eternal advocate in us?

"There is no normal life that
is free of pain. It's the very
wrestling of our problems that
can be the impetus for our
growth."
~ Mr. Rogers, TV Host, Author

Building Resilience and Courage

Children are naturally strong, resilient, adaptable, and resourceful – we can serve as their anchor and encourage them to persevere.

My parents were loving and supportive, but they were also insistent that I have experiences outside our community in south central Los Angeles. My father worked for himself and acted as neighborhood dad, picking up five kids and dropping us off at school. We had many interesting conversations during those rides – he told us stories and taught us about life. Each summer, my parents signed me up for various camps in the beach city communities. In most I was the only African American participant, which made me uncomfortable.

One experience stands out in my mind – a drama camp in Redondo Beach. Again, I was the only African American girl and I felt like everyone else had a friend but me. One day a girl talked to me during a workshop, and I felt so happy – maybe she could be my new friend. That day at lunch I saw her eating with her group, and I got the courage to go over and say hello. When I approached, the main girl said to me, "What are you doing over here?" Mortified, I turned and left, finding a place to sit and eat my lunch alone, once again. That afternoon, I told my mother what happened, in between sobs. This must have been twice as painful for my parents, but they never showed it. They continued to encourage me to persevere and get what I could from the camp. My dad would always tell me, "Tomorrow will be better."

I now have children of my own and realize the importance of providing them with a variety of learning experiences and challenges to overcome. Children are naturally strong, resilient, adaptable, and resourceful, and placing them in situations where these characteristics are allowed to grow is essential to their successful development. Now I realize, thanks to the opportunities provided by my parents, I can walk into any situation with a strong sense of my own self-worth, confident in my ability to communicate and work with a wide range of people. I also feel the experiences I faced helped me to develop a sense of kindness and acceptance toward everyone I approach. ~ Janine Roberts; Age 39; 3 Children; Special Investigator, State of California

Coping skills are valuable tools to share with our children . . .

. . . I know they will inevitably experience grief, trauma, challenges, and setbacks in life—as we all do. What will matter is how they cope. I've helped them develop lots of independent hobbies, so they have many outlets to deal with strong emotions, from crafting to swimming, hiking, surfing, soccer, cycling. Physical exertion works wonders! ~ Lisa Rizzo, Mother of 2

Illness, Disabilities and Developmental Delays Section 9

As your parents we understand
that each of us comes into this world as a unique individual,
with our own genetic gifts and challenges.
Some challenges are greater than others –
they may be apparent early on,
or show themselves in time. . .

We are here for you
no matter what comes our way,
searching out helpful and effective means
of addressing limitations or misfortunes
you may face.

Rest assured, dear one
your life is precious
and we will advocate for you –
doing what we can to help you reach your full potential
and find your place in the world.

We know the only thing we can truly control
is our own mindset,
and we'll do our best
to keep our thoughts and actions
hopeful, constructive, and positive.

Can you feel our love?

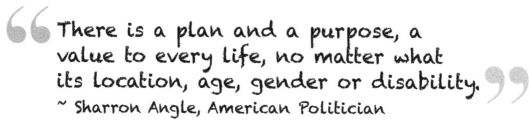

There is a plan and a purpose, a value to every life, no matter what its location, age, gender or disability.
~ Sharron Angle, American Politician

Illness, Disabilities and Developmental Delays

"Our son is now in his early 20s and finishing up four years of college. He is happy, self-sufficient, confident and motivated, and my wife and I are excited to see where life will take him. Reflecting back, I now realize as a parent of an autistic child, the journey first begins with recognizing the situation – acknowledging and processing the feelings of fear, shame, and guilt that we are somehow responsible for this burden our child must carry. As others try to bring the issue to light, parents are likely to feel as if they are being attacked. The key, I believe, is to connect with good information and good people. We have found with absolute certainty that early intervention by informed advocates can have a tremendously positive impact on a young, autistic child." ~ Anonymous Father

Each child is a rare and special pearl on our strand.

As a mom nearing my 70s, I've begun to see my life as a string of pearls. . . before my three children were born, I envisioned having a pure white strand – simple, uniform and perfect. I failed to realize the rarity of a strand of perfectly matching pearls and was surprised when each child's birth brought a luminous pearl of a different color -- one I had never imagined or even known existed.

In nature, pearls come in a vast array of shapes and sizes, colors and hues – all with an iridescent luster which brings with it a special sort of magic. One could say the same of people. My string of pearls, which has grown throughout my lifetime, consists of those closest to me. It is precious – colorful and unique. . .unlike any other. Our third child, a daughter, was born with Down syndrome thirty-three years ago. She is a rare and special pearl on my strand, fastened securely on each side by a sturdy knot. . .holding her place among our family and closest friends.
~ Liz Guho-Johnson; Age 69; 3 Children; Retired Family and Consumer Science Teacher

"Life is the warmth of hearts that are interconnected." ~ Fereydoon Moshiri, Poet

When raising a child with a disability, it's essential to always be your child's advocate.

When my son was diagnosed with ADHD, I read everything I could find on the subject. My research led me to a fantastic occupational therapist who helped us at home. Weighted blankets, auditory training, skin brushing, and exercise were just a few of the helpful techniques which proved highly beneficial. After raising my son and working as a Special Ed teacher for years, my advice to parents is this: "Don't allow other people to make you feel as if your child's disability is your fault, or theirs; learn to separate yourself from the judgment of others, and always be your child's advocate – they must know you have their back." ~ Anonymous, Mother of 2

Growth Mindset Section 10

Little one, you are embarking on an exciting journey ~
one which will encompass your entire lifetime,
as your talents and abilities develop and expand.

Let's choose to look at things through the right lens,
understanding the power and influence
our attitude and mental outlook have
on each experience we encounter.

We will help you to view challenge and change
with excitement and confidence,
secure in the belief that you can grow and succeed.
We'll also do our best to maintain an open and curious mindset ourselves,
and realize there is much to be learned
from circumstances and experiences
outside our areas of comfort and routine.

Can we look for the expansion and beauty in growth, together?

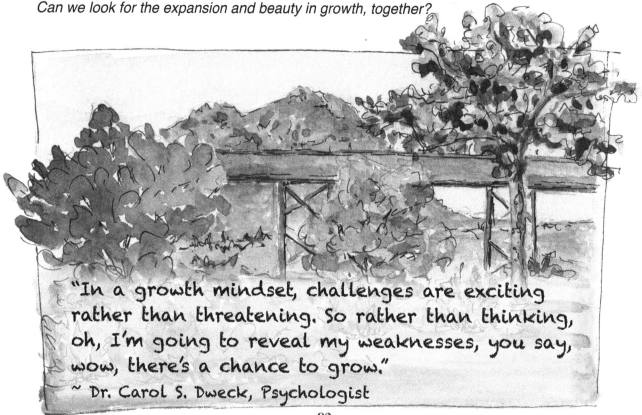

"In a growth mindset, challenges are exciting
rather than threatening. So rather than thinking,
oh, I'm going to reveal my weaknesses, you say,
wow, there's a chance to grow."
~ Dr. Carol S. Dweck, Psychologist

Growth Mindset

Parents and caregivers can foster the development of a "growth mindset" in their children while helping them to realize their full potential.

Researcher and psychologist Carol Dweck has identified two different mindsets in children. In a fixed mindset, children believe that their intelligence, abilities and talents are fixed traits -- they have a certain amount of these and will never have more. This way of thinking limits children and prevents them from trying new things and reaching their full potential. Other kids have a growth mindset about their abilities – they understand the plasticity of their brain and recognize that the more they exercise it, the stronger it becomes. Every time they try hard at something new, their brain forms new connections, which over time will make them more capable and allow them to develop their intelligence! According to Carol Dweck, "If parents want to give their children a gift, the best thing they can do is teach them to love challenges, be intrigued by mistakes, enjoy effort and keep on learning."

One way to help your child develop a growth mindset is by praising and encouraging his or her process and effort, doing your best to be specific. Instead of saying simply, "Good job," consider praising your little one with, "You kept trying and trying to reach that toy, and you grabbed it!" For a toddler who's building a tower of blocks, try, "Even though some blocks kept falling, you stuck with it, and you made this high tower! Look how many blocks you used!" If your older child struggles on a math problem and succeeds, you might comment, "You tried different ways to solve the problem, put in the time and effort, and you did it! Your brain is growing." When your child feels frustrated about a task, try adding the word "yet." For example, "You haven't made a soccer goal *yet*." This simple word helps instill the belief that with effort and perseverance, they can improve, learn, and reach their goals.

Praising children for personal traits such as being smart, pretty, artistic, or athletic helps perpetuate a fixed mindset and an attitude that they cannot improve or change a situation. Recognizing their process and effort gives them the belief that they have a sense of control over their success, motivates them to persevere, and builds resilience. ~ Nadine McCarty; 64; 2 children; Retired Parent Education Instructor

Parents can encourage and model positive self talk!

Patterns of negative or positive self-talk often start in childhood. For as long as I can remember, math was the one subject in school which I struggled with. It didn't take long for me to see myself as being bad at math. I got frustrated easily, and eventually simply stopped trying. As my own children grew, I watched my husband guide and encourage them, helping them to believe they could learn anything if they simply put in the effort. Feeling capable and empowered is a gift we can give our children! ~ Lisa Guy

Chapter 5
Reflections

Notes for Chapter 5 – Refer back for quick reminders!

Chapter 6

Satisfaction and Fulfillment –
What Truly Matters

"The universe buries strange jewels deep within us,
and then stands back to see if we can find them."
~ Elizabeth Gilbert, _Big Magic_[1]

True Wealth

What really matters most in life? Money and expensive possessions may bring happiness for a short time, but without a connection to sentiment or meaning, that feeling is likely to wear off quickly. We can give our children the gift of being a part of a loving community with roots and help them to understand that happiness can be found with the right perspective – from our own contributions, relationships, and experiences, regardless of the amount of money or material possessions we have. Demonstrating the benefits of living a simple, productive life, versus promoting a dream of opulence in later years can help to ensure their own lives are joyful, rewarding, and promising. ~ Lisa Guy

Deep happiness and personal satisfaction come from relationships, and a sense of purpose and self-worth, rather than possessions and material objects.

After several years of saving, I was so happy to finally have a family dining table with 6 matching chairs in a warm, honey maple finish. I envisioned many enjoyable family meals on this table for years to come. My daughter, age four, and I loved to work on small art projects together, usually in the dining room, so we continued creating art on our brand-new table. One day, I was cleaning up after our art play and noticed a gash under the paper where she had worked. The gash was blue, deep, and very pronounced.

I was so disappointed. What was I going to do to fix this marring of our perfect table? Should I sand it down and refinish the surface? I went through a range of emotions until a friend helped me to put it all in perspective. She said: "As your children grow and leave their marks, stains, and chips on your furniture, walls, and other material possessions, think of them as 'love marks' – which are special because they've been touched by your children." Those words found a place in my heart and helped me realize what is truly important in life. It is not the material wealth we accumulate, not the things, or even the prestige or social status we may attain, but rather the people we share our lives with, the contributions and memories we make, the love and knowledge we gain, and the experiences we have. With just a small shift of thinking, the troublesome gouge in our dining room table became something I accepted and even embraced. ~ Cameron Shields; Age 60; 2 Children; Artist and Community Volunteer

Holidays and Rituals Section 1

We will enjoy many special days
throughout your life,
celebrating the seasons, holidays, birthdays
rites of passage and other important occasions.

Maintaining and creating family rituals
and joining together with our community and loved ones
will help to mark these distinctive events.

Let's emphasize time spent together
rather than presents and monetary gifts,
and do our best to relax and be flexible.

We can make good memories for ourselves and future generations
and realize that every moment need not be perfect,
but is certain to be precious.

Won't we have such fun?

"Remember, the best present anyone can give is being there for their loved ones."
~ Unknown

Holidays and Rituals

Continuing the traditions of our ancestors can connect us to our roots and bring us joy.

As a kid, I was awed by the mystery of the holidays, especially the winter ones. What were these special days that had the power to make the whole world stand still? To keep my dad from going to work? To close down the usual places we went for outings, and create an intangible feeling of atmosphere which told my little sister and me, that for a select precious time, nothing else mattered besides a feeling that none could name or say?

Time has passed, my sister and I have grown up, and I notice our longing during the holidays for that lost sense of timelessness. It's harder to find now, yet we endeavor to invite the connecting presence of holiday love back into our lives. Since time immemorial our ancestors have interrupted their daily routines at particular seasonal points, creating a window through which to view the sweet stillness and togetherness underlying human life. Thanks to them, we have trees adorned with lights and stars in our houses, candles in sacred holders, or something else that helps us remember, and connects us to our roots. Gratefully, the ways of our ancestors are still there for us to embrace. We can make the whole world stand still if we choose to imbue it with that kind of imagination, myth, and magic. . . bringing together our family and community in the name of love and joy!

If there's a secret to the magic of holidays, perhaps it's just this: for one day, let the line between imagination and reality become too faint to identify…let the bearded Elder from the north still fly across the sky in a reindeer-led sleigh. For what is more mystical and mysterious than this power of imagination residing in each one of us? ~ Sam McRee; Age 32; Teacher/Naturalist/Author

Maintaining a tradition of honoring family members on birthdays and other special occasions can strengthen family bonds and solidify relationships.

Our family has started a tradition of honoring each other on birthdays, and other special occasions. As we gather for a meal, each family member shares a memory or story about the celebrated individual. Often the memories are humorous, sometimes sentimental, and always special. This time allows us all to reflect on our relationship with one another and the bond we share. Being there for and remembering to appreciate our loved ones is a valuable practice to pass on to our children. ~ Lisa Guy

Morals and Values Section 2

My child, as you grow,
we know that what we do
will be more important than what we say.

We will do our best
to model good morals and values,
sharing with you
honesty and fairness,
caring and compassion,
generosity and loyalty,
as well as the art of being polite and respectful,
and the ability to practice
self-control, integrity, and perseverance.

Let's help each other, shall we?

"When my son was born, our pediatrician said something that would stay with me forever: 'As you raise him, make sure he develops a conscience, and everything else will follow from there.'"
~ Lauryn Niezen,
Mother of 2

Morals and Values

Having both parents on the same page is crucial – we turn off our cell phones when we're home with our family and do our best to stay present. It's important to us that our children learn good morals and values. We don't care if they are great scholars or exceptional athletes – what matters most to us is that they have good manners and grow to be respectful, responsible adults. ~ Cherisse Sweeney, Mother of 2

☆ ☆ ☆

It's never too late to work on values such as honesty, integrity, and compassion.

Strong morals and values are the building blocks of a healthy society and play an essential role in forming stable communities - they are also one of the greatest gifts we can give our children. Our own moral code or blueprint has been developing our entire lives, passed on from our parents, and their parents before them. The experiences we've had, along with socialization from our families, schools, and culture, have shaped us irrevocably. It's never too late to work on values such as honesty, integrity, and compassion.

The most effective way to teach our children, is to demonstrate critical concepts by incorporating them into our daily lives. Young people do not respond well to lecturing, but closely watch what we do and how we treat others. Listening to our children, speaking to them in a quiet, respectful voice, and talking to them during meals, after story time or at bedtime, usually finds them receptive and ready to listen and learn. We can encourage them to be critical thinkers through literature and film, providing an opportunity to develop questions and formulate their own solutions. How did the characters behave? Would they want the characters as friends? Why or why not? ~ Leslie Rotstein; Age 80; 3 children, 7 grandchildren, 3 great-grandchildren, past Teacher, Business Owner, current Mentor and Nonprofit Director

☆ ☆ ☆

We can aspire to teach our children to be kind with the ability to see beyond themselves.

As a 7th grade teacher, I have the pleasure of interacting with students who are smart, funny, athletic, artistic and/or musical. I appreciate these qualities but the students that stand out the most are those who are kind and able to see beyond themselves. As parents, we can look for talents and strengths in our children and help them to find ways of contributing to our society. It is so easy to be selfish, but teaching kindness, consideration for others, and the value of contributing to the greater good should be high on a parent's priority list. It's good to remember that we all benefit when we help others. ~ Jenna Porchia, Mother of 2

Child Care Considerations Section 3

Little one,
many adventures lie ahead.
We will make sure you are safe
and well taken care of, always.

As you grow,
you will have a variety of experiences,
meet many new friends,
and develop your own sense of self,
separate from our family.

You will learn to trust others
and see how you can make a positive impact
wherever you are.

Be assured,
we can be relied upon
and will always be there for you.

Do you know how much you mean to us?

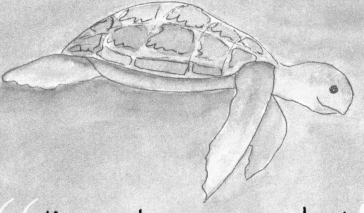

Mama always comes back.
~ Jamie Funderburk, Public Health
Nurse, Mother of 2

Child Care Considerations

Our children are our most precious gifts. If we know we will resume working outside the home after Baby's arrival, it is a good idea to spend time and energy before the birth, to secure childcare in alignment with our and our partner's priorities, giving us both peace of mind. Young children develop quickly and should receive loving care closely mirroring that which they receive at home. Research shows that the experiences a child has during the first five years will have a significant impact on long-term development. Remember to think outside the box – brainstorm with your partner, parents, grandparents, extended family, friends and work associates, to see if you can come up with a child care arrangement and schedule which accommodates both you and your new little one. Having this done in advance will reduce a great deal of stress after the baby comes. ~ Lisa Guy

Our children benefit when we are proactive and take time to do our research when looking for an appropriate child care provider.

Before our first child was born, my husband and I had just purchased a new business, in addition to our first home. I was an educator and knew I would need to return to work not long after our son's birth, so I did my research beforehand, and thankfully was able to secure a great child care provider. The woman we found was the wife of someone my husband had known for years. She had a long, stellar track record, but I still spent time making calls, checking references, and finding out as much about her as I could. Thank goodness I had done my research! When our son was just one month old, my husband went on a trip with his buddies and had a serious accident. Because we had our child care lined up in advance, I was able to go back to work sooner than planned, and a great deal of additional stress was eliminated. ~ Anonymous, Mother of 4

At the end of the day, each child should feel loved and valued.

As a Teaching Principal at a new Head Start facility in the desert, I was adamant that each of our aides welcome every child with eye contact, and a friendly smile and greeting using the child's name. Aides were also to engage with the children throughout the day, using soft, caring language. If a child was experiencing stress, the aides were to kneel down to the child's level, provide undivided attention, and show their concerns were being heard. I also liked to remind parents that when leaving a child at school or with a babysitter or daycare provider, it's always a good idea to tell them when they will be picked up, as well as who will be coming to get them.
~ Leslie Rotstein, Age 80; 3 Children; 7 Grandchildren; 3 Great-grandchildren; past Teacher, Business Owner

"I believe in the importance of hello and good-bye rituals - when I drop my boys off at school, I always blow them a kiss as they turn and wave to me. . .and when their dad picks them up from school, I make sure I'm waiting at the door to give them a big hug when they return!"
~ Aubrey Semenova; Age 32; 3 Children; Registered Nurse

Inclusiveness and Collaboration Section 4

Did you know,
that a strong sense of connectedness
to people and places
brings happiness and joy?

We will do our best
to bring people together
whenever possible
and to work cohesively
within our community
and the greater world.

There is power in numbers!

> **If you want to go fast, go alone.
> If you want to go far, go together.**
>
> ~ African Proverb

Inclusiveness and Collaboration

"…we all have the capacity to transcend self-interest and become simply a part of a whole. It's not just a capacity; it's the portal to many of life's most cherished experiences."
~ Johnathan Haidt, The Righteous Mind[2]

INCLUSIVENESS

Being included feels good to adults and children alike.

Most people are social by nature and happiest when part of a group. Being included feels good, bringing a sense of comfort, stability, and peace. Parents of medically fragile children have an especially challenging time, and it has been beautiful to see these parents, supported by our nonprofit, Jack's Helping Hand, celebrate the joys and accomplishments of their kids with other like-minded parents. Most kids have an opportunity to participate in various sports, clubs, and other extracurricular activities, but children with severe illnesses or disabilities have fewer chances to have these experiences. Their parents miss out as well. Providing quality social, emotional, and growth opportunities for our kids at Jack's Helping Hand fills many of these unmet needs. I've seen fast friendships develop for both parents and children, as they participate in joyful events like parades, riding and swimming programs, camps, and Christmas parties, bringing families together to more fully celebrate life. ~ Bridget Ready; Age 62; 4 Children; Retired Elementary Teacher; Nonprofit Founder

COLLABORATION

Collaboration begins with having an open mindset – inviting input and being willing to give most anything a try, if it aligns with our objectives!

I've worked as a Secondary Vice Principal for a number of schools in our district over the past 7 years. What has struck me the hardest is the need to unify cooperatively as a group to effect change. At our elementary school, thirteen different languages are spoken! We celebrate our differences, and come together cohesively, with the school slogan, "Together We Shine!" I look for ways to collaborate. What are other schools doing to encourage camaraderie, acceptance, learning, and engagement? How can I bring our school community together, effectively, fostering strong relationships and encouraging teachers, parents, students, and staff to experience the sense of being part of a close-knit, supportive group? I believe the place to begin is to have an open mindset. I invite input and am willing to give anything a try if it seems likely to help with our mission: promoting unity, inclusivity, and student growth. This mindset opens the door to opportunity, encourages others to join the team, and empowers all to participate in our school community. ~ Aaron Black; Age 44; 2 Children; Elementary School Principal

Motivation From Within and Finding Purpose Section 5

Dear one,
some of us develop a sense of purpose on our own early in life,
and others need a little help from those around them.

We will do our best to make sure you have
lots of experiences and choices throughout your childhood,
along with opportunities to grow and develop confidence in your abilities.

We'll give ongoing feedback balanced with specific praise,
encourage your efforts and interest in many areas,
and share your enthusiasm as you master new skills.
These actions will help to develop your sense of self,
purpose, and inner compass –
qualities instrumental in attaining a rewarding life.

What will you be motivated by?

"The greatest good you can do
for another is not just share
your riches, but reveal to them
their own."
~ Benjamin Disraeli (1804-1881),
British Writer, Politician

Motivation From Within and Finding Purpose

Intrinsic motivation exists in children when they are excited about learning, interested in acquiring new skills, and eager to explore new topics.

My husband and I have taught for 8 and 10 years, respectively. We understand how different all children are from each other - what motivates them, what they're drawn to, the style of learning that works best for them. . . we also understand the importance of providing young people with many opportunities to participate in learning. It's important to connect with them and help them feel good about themselves when they succeed - not just because they've won an award or received a good grade (extrinsic motivators) but simply because their success gives them a feeling of satisfaction. Inviting kids to have a voice in discussions and making them feel like they have a part in the learning process further aids in the establishment of their intrinsic motivation.

Our first born has always been talkative and confident and we've tried to foster her interests and faith in her abilities through encouragement, undivided attention and by providing resources to help her continue to learn and grow. This approach has contributed to her progress over the past 4 ½ years – she loves reading, writing, drawing, crafting, and trying new, challenging things! We were amazed when she began speaking in sentences by her first birthday and could sing several songs at 15 months. Our son is 1, and currently attends daycare. We do not see the same advanced language in him yet, but we continue to encourage him to embrace challenges, persevere through hard times, and take his time while learning new content and mastering new skills. ~ Jenna Porchia; Age 32; 2 Children, Teacher

☆   ☆   ☆

Fostering intrinsic motivation in our children by helping them to explore interests as well as set and accomplish goals, will likely bring them satisfaction and fulfillment.

From an early age I was fascinated by all things mechanical – how did a clock keep the time. . . where did the sounds come from inside a music box . . . how did a computer function? I took apart many things when I was young, trying my best to figure out what made them work, and how they could be reassembled or modified.

With my own children, I have done my best to foster their intrinsic motivation, talking to them at length about a wide variety of subjects, noticing areas which interest them and guiding and encouraging their exploration and mastery of these subjects. My wife and I did our best to avoid trying to motivate them with external rewards or punishments. Instead, we encouraged hard work and accomplishments for the pure joy of doing well and feeling proud of a job well done. Thinking back, I realize I've never been motivated by outside factors. The desire to pursue areas of intrigue and conquer challenges has greatly overshadowed any interest I've had in making money or receiving accolades. My reward has been in the satisfaction I've obtained from following my passions and accomplishing my goals. ~ Keith Guy; Age 62; 5 Children; Retired Entrepreneur and Roboticist

Responsibility, Work Ethic and Self-Sufficiency Section 6

Little one,
we each carry the responsibility
of finding our unique place in the world.

We all come with our respective gifts
and contributions to make,
and we will do our best to help you realize yours!

There can be such joy
in working hard,
learning, growing, celebrating,
and sharing what we accomplish.
This gives us a strong sense of satisfaction
and self-fulfillment.

We are so excited to be alongside you on this journey!

"Chores are the key to responsibility - start as soon as your child can walk. Chores will help them feel important, a part of the family, and will allow them to develop a sense of confidence and order early on."
~ Lynn Stafford, Mother of 3

Responsibility, Work Ethic and Self-Sufficiency

"Self-motivation generally doesn't happen overnight. It takes a certain amount of discipline and perseverance on our part, but there is no doubt that when we give our children jobs and projects and show our confidence in their abilities to follow through and complete them, long term benefits will appear!" ~ Margaux O'Quest, Mother of 3

Teaching our children the correlation between focused time, hard work and success can empower them to be confident, responsible, and self-sufficient.

Growing up with a young, single mother and a mixed racial background definitely had its challenges. Our apartment was in a dangerous part of town, in California's Central Valley, and I saw a lot of rough things when I was young. Fortunately, I always knew my mom, grandma and grandpa loved me and had my back. My mom told me from a young age that I had choices, and if I wanted to have a good life, I needed to work hard for it.

I am now a physics and chemistry teacher back at my old high school, and it gives me such pleasure to inspire and empower my students to believe in themselves and their ability to work hard to accomplish great things! My teaching technique has evolved over the years. I believe that science is the perfect subject to teach investigative skills, independent thinking, and individual empowerment. Rather than expecting my students to carry out lab experiments with heavily prescribed instructions, I give them a project with enough knowledge to explore scientific studies on their own and try different methods to arrive at a desired outcome. Learning the principles of chemistry and physics and understanding how to apply them can provide a great deal of personal satisfaction! If students are stuck, I'll come over to their lab group and start asking questions . . . Have they thought about giving this a try. . .? What would happen if they did this. . .?

I've also found great benefits in assessing each student when the class first begins, and then testing again a few weeks in. The first test establishes a baseline, and the second shows how far they've come in just a short time. Then I'm able to explain how much more can be accomplished if they continue to work hard throughout the class. Regardless of their aptitude for science, showing students how much of an impact focused time and hard work have on their success is paramount. ~ Anthony Porchia; Age 31; 2 Children; High School Physics and Chemistry Teacher

"As a long-time teacher and mother of three, advice from Judith Martin's book, <u>Miss Manners' Guide to Rearing Perfect Children</u>[3], has stayed with me for many years: When traveling with children, always make them responsible for carrying their own things."
~ Juliane McAdam, Mother of 3

Fostering Curiosity, Imagination, Creativity, & Passion Section 7

As a toddler
you will learn about the world around you
by touching, smelling, hearing, tasting, and seeing things.

We will help you to be a curious learner and unearth your passions
by looking for ways to provide hands-on experiences
with opportunities for purposeful activity
and problem solving throughout your childhood.

Imaginary play, positive affirmations which strengthen your confidence,
stories with you as the main character,
unscheduled time spent in nature and at home,
as well as guidance in learning to follow your intuition,
will all help to develop your creativity and passion for life and learning.

The possibilities are endless!

" *A love of learning is the very best quality we can foster in our children. We can take them to the beach, library, aquarium, or museum. . . answer their questions, notice what they're drawn to, and follow their lead. Every child develops at his or her own pace – we can look for their "window" to open, and it will be apparent when they are ready to learn. Staying positive, encouraging, and fun will ensure the best possible experience for everyone!* "

~Robin Reed, Grandmother, Mother of 2, Preschool Owner/Teacher

Fostering Curiosity, Imagination, Creativity, and Passion

 Creating stories for our children with them as the main character can encourage creativity, imagination and empowerment.

For years now, I have been creating imaginary stories for our three young grandchildren. One of our favorite pastimes has been to settle on the couch together while I tell them stories (with themselves as the main characters) as they adventure through various trials and exciting quests – always coming out victorious! This past Christmas I wrote each of them several stories and made them into a book. They could not have been more excited. I believe this activity has not only brought us all much closer, but helps to instill imagination, confidence, excitement and the idea that anything is possible – we simply must imagine it!
~ Bob Owen; Age 69; 2 Children; 3 Grandchildren; Retired Psychiatrist

☆ ☆ ☆

"If you only do what you can do, you'll always be what you are. The more experience a child has with real purposeful activity and solving problems, the more useful, creative, and effective her imagination will become." ~ Susan Stephenson, The Joyful Child[4]

☆ ☆ ☆

 Parents can model the process of finding their own passions while guiding their maturing children to do the same.

A starting point for unearthing our deepest desires is to spend time daydreaming or journaling, and then create an action plan which outlines the areas we believe to be of the greatest importance. It is helpful to group dreams into specific categories such as personal growth, vocation, home and family, health, social responsibility, and spiritual enlightenment. The next step is to turn dreams into goal statements. If you remember to call your purpose and goals into your consciousness as often as possible, you'll be on the path to finding your passion. Take your goals and purpose with you throughout each day…eat with them, sleep with them, and share them with others. In this way, your passion will grow steadily and eventually become your reality. My young 12-year-old friend embodies this process perfectly. She eats, sleeps, and breathes her art. Not long ago, her art teacher suggested she invest in a computer – set up a website and start selling her work. She recently showed me one of her pieces and I was so blown away by it, I asked if I could buy it from her. She was thrilled at the idea. She framed it for me, and it is now proudly displayed in my healing room." ~ Hilary Anderson, Age 66; Teacher/Coach/Licensed Spiritual Healer

☆ ☆ ☆

"Creativity is so delicate a flower that praise tends to make it bloom while discouragement often nips it in the bud." ~ Alex F. Osborn, Father of "Brainstorming"

Hope Section 8

My love,
hope is something we must strive for
throughout our lives.
It gives us comfort, motivation,
encouragement, and determination.

As long as there is life, there is hope.

"Hope is the thing with feathers, that perches in the soul, and sings the tune without the words, and never stops at all."
~ Emily Dickinson, Poet

Hope

When faced with tremendous hardship, we can choose to focus on all of our blessings and hold onto hope.

When the pregnancy test came back positive, we were ecstatic! God had blessed us with a third child!! I had hoped and prayed for more children but was not sure what was in store for us. Rewind to three months earlier, the doctor had called. Cancer, she told us. I, a 28-year-old wife and mother of two children under 3, had cancer. I could have no more children, and this news devastated me. My husband, family, friends, and I were stunned. We didn't know what to do, so we prayed. We prayed, long and hard, and through many tears, I came to peace with my diagnosis. I had so much hope for our future!

I hoped to see my daughter start dancing. I hoped to see my son going to work with his daddy. I hoped to have my children help me in the kitchen…with chores around the house… and I hoped to teach them so many lessons in life. Rather than focusing on what could be, or the struggles we would face ahead, I chose to focus on all of the blessings I had.

As my doctors helped determine the best course of treatment, a miracle was revealed – I was pregnant! Several of the doctors were very concerned, and suggested that I terminate the pregnancy, but I knew this was something I could never do… I hoped and prayed my new baby and I would make it through cancer together. Amazingly, not only did we make it through, but we thrived! Hope and faith in God's plans kept me from fearing what might be, made me peaceful and excited about our family's future, and allowed me to appreciate everything I was going through: pain, suffering, growth, and joy.

It's been 2 years from my diagnosis and treatment and I am now cancer free with three beautiful children, one of whom is a healthy one-year-old boy. Believing in something greater than ourselves, having faith in the future, and holding on to hope, make all the difference as we move forward with our lives. ~ Ashley Loweree; Age 30; 3 Children; former Teaching Student, current Stay-at-Home Mama

Collective hopes for the future are shared and involve the entire family.

"…I had to stop and look inside myself, rather than concentrate on all that was going on around me. When I gave myself that time, I realized that my hopes involved not only me but also my family. So my wife and I developed a set of hopes together. These hopes included aspirations such as being in balance with ourselves, contributing to and supporting a positive spirit of community, sustaining financial flexibility, being healthy and happy, finding peace in what we feel called to do, and living abundantly amid uncertainty. Articulating your Hopes is the first step to living them." ~ Don Maruska, How Great Decisions Get Made[5]

Given Wings, Where Will You Fly? Section 9

Little one,
we come into this world as distinct individuals ~
with our own unique qualities, tendencies, and gifts
and the daily care, experiences, and learning opportunities provided us
greatly affect our growth and development.

A strong foundation built on love, honesty, trust, and support,
combined with good habits, positive role modeling,
and a balance of discipline and freedom,
will empower you to become a caring, capable, self-sufficient,
and contributing adult.

At times we may feel like you'll need our steadfast support forever,
and yet we must remember our time with you is finite
. . . and each moment is precious.

Let's make the most of your childhood years, months, days, and moments
while we continue to learn and explore the world together,
preparing you for your time to fly.

Though the days may feel long, the years are decidedly short. . .

"As your parents, we must
remember that although we
brought you into this world
and will love, nurture, and
guide you, your
life is not ours
to keep."

~ Nisha AbdulCader,
Pediatrician, Mother
of 4

Given Wings, Where Will You Fly?

Parents are a child's most important champion. With unconditional love and the right nurturing and guidance, we can help them find their own inner strength, step back, and watch them fly!

As the years pass, I've become increasingly aware of the many gifts I've received throughout my lifetime. I was fortunate to have a strong, caring family with parents who took an interest in my education, helped me to establish good habits early on, and provided me with many experiences, love, and support throughout my life.

For 29 years my husband and I had at least one child at home, needing our help and guidance . . . keeping us company. We simply weren't prepared for our youngest to leave for college. When he left, the void we felt was vast.

My aging father was living with us at the time in a small apartment we had crafted at the back of our house, and the day my husband and I returned from settling our son into his new college dormitory, my father walked into our kitchen and said, "You have an empty nest!" And my husband replied, "Well actually, Ron, we still have you." And with a scowl on his face, my father replied, "You have an OLD egg!!!"

Oh, I was so grateful to have that "old egg" still with us at home. As my father's health declined, he spoke more and more about his childhood. He told me stories about his early years growing up in a small town in Wisconsin with his five siblings and hard-working Italian mother and father. I treasured those stories. . . I treasure them still.

Toward the end, my father allowed me to care for him for the first time in his life - he was a proud man who never wanted to accept help from anyone. As I sat on the edge of his bed, I sang him to sleep and suddenly understood the cycle of life, as he had done the same for me so many years ago, sitting patiently with his large, warm hand on the small of my back, singing me lullabies each night as I drifted off, peacefully.

Those who offer the best of themselves to their children may find it reflected back to them when they need it most.

~ Lisa Guy, Mother of 5

A Thought to Leave You With...

"Gratitude unlocks the fullness of life. It turns what we have into enough, and more. It turns denial into acceptance, chaos to order, confusion to clarity. It can turn a meal into a feast, a house into a home, a stranger into a friend. Gratitude makes sense of our past, brings peace for today, and creates a vision for tomorrow." ~ Melody Beattie

I am so grateful for you, my precious child.

Chapter 6
Reflections

Notes for Chapter 6 – Refer back for quick reminders!

Acknowledgments

This book was a true collaboration and would not have been possible without the help of many people. Thank you, Cammy Shields, for contributing your precious artwork which transformed Pearls into something naturally inviting and engaging. I am grateful for each and every person who shared a story, message or quote – your knowledge, experience and perspective will help many new parents and caregivers. I have been so fortunate to have the editing expertise of Mary Pellegrino, Rita Mathern, Maliena Guy, Jenna Porchia, Marie McRee and Sally Vito! Thank you to Addie Vanden Bossche, Dr. Kathleen Long, Dr. Nisha Abdul Cader, Ana O'Sullivan, Lea Payne Scott, Lisa Boyd, Liz Guho-Johnson, Nara Clark, Irene Chadwick, and Juliane McAdam, for spending time reviewing sections and giving helpful input. Parent participation teachers Nadine McCarty and Denise Indvik have provided invaluable feedback and outstanding local connections, and Trish Avery from the United Way took the time to read through the pages and share helpful suggestions. To my graphic artist, Kate Summers – you could not have been more fun to work with, and your creative abilities have made an indelible mark on the book! Leslie Rotstein, Don Maruska and Lisa Fraser – thank you for meeting with me early on in the writing process, and being generous with your time and encouragement. Much gratitude to Christine Kimball for starting the process by saying several years ago, "Lisa, you should write a book!" And finally, thank you to my dear friend, Patti Cook, for your unyielding enthusiasm and support, and to my husband Keith and children, for showing me how rewarding a compassionate, loving and committed family can be.

Resources

Introduction

1. Importance of Early Communication link: https://www.zerotothree.org/resource/how-to-support-your-childs-communication-skills/

Chapter 1 – Parenting of Infants

1. Important Resource for Parents: https://www.healthychildren.org.
2. Product recall website: https://www.safekids.org/Product-Recalls.
3. Davies, Simone. *The Montessori Toddler*. Workman Publishing, 2019.
4. La Leche League website: https://www.llli.org.
5. Chapman, Gary D., and Ross Campbell. *The 5 Love Languages of Children: The Secret to Loving Children Effectively*. Moody Publishers, 2016.

Chapter 2 – Early Practices

1. Brown, Brené. *Atlas of the Heart*. Random House Publishing, 2021.
2. Second Step website: https://www.secondstep.org/.
3. Gewirtz, Abigail. *When the World Feels Like a Scary Place*. Workman Publishing, 2020.
4. Postpartum Support International (PSI) link: https://www.postpartum.net.
5. Maruska, Don, and Jay Perry. *Take Charge of Your Talent*. Berrett-Koehler Publishers, 2013.

Chapter 3 – Authoritative (or Heart-Centered) Parenting/Good Habits

1. Chapman, Gary D., and Ross Campbell. *The 5 Love Languages of Children: The Secret to Loving Children Effectively*. Moody Publishers, 2016.
2. Five Senses Breathing link: https://www.yourtherapysource.com>blog1/2020/07/03-5-sensesgroundingexercise.
3. Davies, Simone. *The Montessori Toddler*. Workman Publishing, 2019.
4. Chödrön, Pema. *Living Beautifully*. Shambala Publications, 2012.
5. Lansbury, Janet. *No Bad Kids*. Self-Published, 2014.

6. Gewirtz, Abigail. *When the World Feels Like a Scary Place*. Workman Publishing, 2020.

7. POSAFY website: https://www.posafy.org.

8. Policy Statement, American Academy of Pediatrics, Media and Young Minds, 2016 link: https://publications.aap.org/pediatrics/article/138/5/e20162591/60503/Media-and-Young-Minds

9. Parenting Styles link: https://www.parentingforbrain.com/4-baumrind-parenting-styles/.

10. Positive Discipline link: https://www.positivediscipline.com/.

11. Hatfield, Linda and Ty, and Wendy Thomas Russell. *ParentShift*. Brown Paper Press Publishing, 2019.

12. Siegel, Daniel J., and Tina Payne Bryson. *No-Drama Discipline - The Whole-Brain Way to Calm the Chaos and Nurture Your Child's Developing Mind*. Bantam Books Publishing, 2016.

Chapter 4 – Raising Connected Children

1. Fogg, BJ. *Tiny Habits: The Small Changes that Change Everything*. Houghton Mifflin Harcourt Publishing, 2020.

2. Chapman, Gary D., and Ross Campbell. *The 5 Love Languages of Children: The Secret to Loving Children Effectively*. Moody Publishers, 2016.

3. Five Protective Factors link: https://familynurturingcenter.org/5-protective-factors/.

4. Siegel, Daniel J., and Tina Payne Bryson. *The Whole-Brain Child: Revolutionary Strategies to Nurture Your Child's Developing Mind*. Delacorte Press, 2011.

5. Hatfield, Linda and Ty, and Wendy Thomas Russell. *ParentShift*. Brown Paper Press Publishing, 2019.

Chapter 5 – Life Perspective

1. CDC Milestone checklist link: https://www.cdc.gov>ncbddd>actearly>milestones>index.html.

2. American Academy of Pediatrics Healthy Children website link: https://www.healthychildren.org.

3. Chapman, Gary D., and Ross Campbell. *The 5 Love Languages of Children: The Secret to Loving Children Effectively*. Moody Publishers, 2016.

4. Martin, William. *The Parent's Tao Te Ching*. Marlowe & Company Publishing, 1999.

5. Temperament link: http://csefel.vanderbilt.edu/resources/training_ infant.html.

6. Milne, A. A. *Winnie-the-Pooh*. E. P. Dutton Publishing, 1926.

Chapter 6 – Satisfaction and Fulfillment

1. Gilbert, Elizabeth. *Big Magic: Creative Living Beyond Fear*. Riverhead Books, 2015.

2. Haidt, Jonathan. *The Righteous Mind: Why Good People Are Divided by Politics and Religion*. Vintage Publishing, 2012.

3. Martin, Judith. *Miss Manners' Guide to Rearing Perfect Children*. Touchstone Publishing, 2022.

4. Stephenson, Susan. *The Joyful Child*. Michael Olaf Montessori Publishing Company, 2013.

5. Maruska, Don. *How Great Decisions Get Made*. Self-Published, 2004.

About The Author

Lisa Guy is a graduate of UC San Diego with a BA in Communications, a past business co-owner and mother of five. From a young age, Lisa has had an interest in people and their development – especially young children. After her third child was born, she stopped working outside the home and immersed herself in the lives of little ones. During her 30 years of volunteer work as a room parent, classroom volunteer, field trip chaperon, PTA and booster club leader, fundraising chair, teacher/administrative aide, and community volunteer, she became passionate about finding ways to help young people reach their full potential. This book is a culmination of her efforts and experiences. Her belief in the collaborative process has brought many voices together to exemplify a myriad of ideas and valuable parenting principles. These principles were learned through direct contact with children and families, books, classes on parenting, and lived experience with her own five children. Lisa believes that the best way to insure that a child will develop into a happy and productive adult is to have committed and supportive parents/caregivers and community, whom he or she can trust, speak to, and learn from throughout the childhood years.

About The Illustrator

From an early age, Cameron Shields worked alongside her father in his art studio, as he fulfilled his responsibilities as Art Director for an advertising firm. Ever-encouraging of her interest in the study of nature, he spent time with her walking and collecting samples of pond water, leaves, flowers, and other remnants of nature which they examined at home under a microscope, and Cammy spent hours analyzing and drawing. After a career in healthcare and then later teaching science at the university level, Cammy resumed her passion for connecting with nature and exploring her environment through art, and began the practices of birdwatching and watercolor painting. Her whimsical illustrations are a result of her explorations, and bring readers on a meditative journey along California's Central Coast.

Author's Note

In the eleven years between my first and last child, I have observed a marked increase in the level of anxiety and stress of both children and their parents. Increased competition for college admission, social media pressures, the distraction of video games, accessibility and acceptance of drugs, and a polarized political climate have all contributed to a decline in overall mental health and wellbeing. Pearls Parenting Practices has been written with the intent of providing support and guidance to parents, who in turn can help their children to grow and thrive. Parents and caregivers can offer their children the best possible chance in life by establishing a strong foundation of trust and mutual respect early on. It is my hope that reading *Pearls* together will help to build this relationship from the very beginning.